THE STORY OF
GRASS-TRACK RACING
1950-65

THE STORY OF
GRASS-TRACK RACING
1950-65

Robert Bamford & Dave Stallworthy

TEMPUS

First published 2004

Tempus Publishing Ltd
The Mill, Brimscombe Port
Stroud, Gloucestershire GL5 2QG
www.tempus-publishing.com

British Library Cataloguing in Publication Data.
A catalogue record for this book is available from the British Library.

ISBN 0 7524 2838 1

Typesetting and origination by Tempus Publishing.
Printed and bound in Great Britain.

CONTENTS

ACKNOWLEDGEMENTS

To make this publication possible, several wonderful people have had an input and we would like to express our eternal gratitude. Kicking-off then, with a big 'thank you' to John Ogden, who has been quite superb in answering queries at the drop of a hat, and an absolute mine of information, especially with the supplying of results for each year's roll of honour. Without John's incredible knowledge we simply wouldn't be able to give such a clear picture of the history of our sport. Not only did John offer much advice, he also supplied a large amount of photographs and spent many hours cross-checking our work and pointing us in the right direction! We are also indebted to top commentator and *Motor Cycle News* journalist Bob Light, who has supplied excellent images from ace photographers Bill Cole and John Miller, as well as many from his own collection. Special thanks are due to Gordon Francis, and it really is a coup to have the backing of such a renowned photographer for this, the 1950-1965 story – he is certainly a magic lensman indeed! Regrettably, due to the sheer volume of photographs kindly loaned by so many wonderful friends, we found it impossible to use them all. Much appreciation is due to Glynn Shailes and John Jarvis, who have done much to help with the compilation of this publication. Acknowledgement is also due to several other good people, namely Bob Hart, Jack Agnew and Johnny Kelly for helping with information on racing in Ireland; Pete Hawes for supplying photographs and details of grass-track activity at Stokenchurch; and Mick Nokes for providing images and information on the South-East, plus much help via his column in *Speedway Star*.

Dave Stallworthy and Robert Bamford
May 2004

TRIBUTE TO GORDON FRANCIS

Throughout the history of grass-track racing there have been many top photographers, but one man who really stood out from the late 1950s to 1967 was Gordon Francis from Dorset. His fabulous shots appeared in many publications during that time, including the *Motor Cycle News*. Gordon coupled his interest in photography with racing Mini Cooper's, and it was to the four-wheelers that he went solely in the late 1960s. Nearly thirty years on, in the 1990s, he returned to capturing images of bike action, particularly scrambles, trials and grass-track racing, and there is no doubting he is the present number one for taking photographs of the classic scene. Gordon published a book entitled *Bikes, Camera, Action* which was a sell out and plans are afoot for a follow up! He is also part of a consortium that has launched a monthly magazine, covering present-day classic scrambles, trials and grass-track action. Over the years he has taken thousands of pictures in the South and South-West, and if any readers would like to purchase shots of the grass-track greats or club riders, then Gordon is the man to contact. Whether it be Coffin, Godden, Hagon, Kessell, Tatum, Evans, Vincent or Norcutt he has caught them all in action! So, if you would like to build up your collection of photographs from the 1950s and 1960s, please contact Gordon Francis on 01747 822363.

INTRODUCTION

Grass-track racing, the sister sport of speedway, has always produced wheel-to-wheel action from leather-clad gladiators and many fantastic racing exploits that could have easily been lost in the mists of time. Robert Bamford and I are doing something to keep the history of the sport alive. This is the second book in a series on grass-track racing, following on from our first volume, published in 2002, which covered the years 1927-1949. Our long-term plan, hopefully with the blessing of Tempus Publishing, is to take the series right the way through to present times. In each book we bring the reader details of meetings, a yearly roll of honour, race results (including the National Championships which started in 1951) and some very rare photographs and programme illustrations.

It had always been my intention to do something a bit special like this, and having Tempus Publishing involved, along with prolific speedway author Robert Bamford waving his magic wand over my notes and turning them into flowing text, as well as augmenting the story through his vast knowledge, has been simply fantastic.

In a link with the era covered in this volume, I readily admit to being awestruck by what I saw when I was lucky enough to be invited to co-commentate at Rhodes Minnis in 2003. Indeed, I was highly privileged to meet and interview many of the greats who raced during the period covered in the book, including Reg Luckhurst, Tony Black, Denys Goodacre, Dick Barton, Gerry Wheeler, Mervyn Price, Stan Luck, John Britcher, Andy Ross, John Shears, Graham Hancox, Roy Woollard, George Cross, Dave Palmer and Bill Barley. For anyone who wishes to see just what a fabulous circuit this is, the 2003 meeting was actually filmed by a gentleman called Bob Ruffle and he can be contacted on 01795 536872.

For anyone who might be wondering, the superb cover shot on this volume features Denys Goodacre (57) leading from George Bewley (96) during a meeting at Long Newnton. Finally, I would like to apologize in advance should any of the detective work in this volume subsequently prove to be erroneous.

Dave Stallworthy
(Tel. 01454 321694)
May 2004

1
GRASS-TRACK RACING
1950

Following the post-war boom year, 1950 was to witness the start of a slight decline in the fortunes of the British grass-track racing scene. With the loss of Brands Hatch to a road-race circuit, coupled with a particularly wet season, crowds decreased in size, but at least there was still some tremendous racing.

The action got underway with planned events scattered around the UK in April, including those run by the Oswestry & District Motor Club at Mile End Field, Shrewsbury Road, Shropshire; Newcastle & District Motor Club at Woolsington Airfield, Newcastle upon Tyne; Port Sunlight Motorcycle Club at Bebbington, Cheshire; and Bridgnorth & District Motor Club at Swancote. Other clubs were busy organizing meetings too, and these included Hinckley South, Norwich Vikings, Burford, Leicester Query, Leatherhead and King's Norton.

The Norwich Vikings event was of the mountain-style, with E. Walton (JAP Special) taking victory in a brace of finals and also finishing as runner-up in the 350cc and Novice races, with the team competition being won by Ipswich. Meanwhile, the early-season meeting run by the King's Norton Club saw B. Boult emerge as the winner of the 125cc solo race, mounted on a BSA, with the other classes resulting as follows:

> 350cc final – First: Dick Tolley, Second: Jim Cashmore, Third: Peter Moss.
> 500cc final – First: Oliver Bevan, Second: Jim Cashmore, Third: Peter Moss.
> Unlimited final – First: Dick Tolley, Second: Oliver Bevan, Third: Ron Pritchard.
> 600cc Sidecar final – First: Bill Boddice, Second: George Brethick,
>   Third: Sid Hall.
> Unlimited Sidecar final – First: F.G. Carrington, Second: Bill Boddice,
>   Third: T.G. Wykes.

It is interesting to note how British motorcycles dominated at the early events, with BSA, Norton, Royal Enfield, Ariel and, of course, the famous JAP all featuring strongly. Of the riders, Bill Boddice was later to go on to road-race stardom, while Dick Tolley was to go down in history the following year as the first 500cc National Champion.

Each ACU Centre had its top riders, not least in the North-West and Cheshire areas, where the Grindley brothers, Harry Terretta, Ernie Wood, Bob Parker, Ralph Ellison and Vic Masefield were the main men. Among the clubs organizing racing in 1950 were

Sidecar racing at Burford, 1950.

Nantwich, South Liverpool, Wrexham, Broughton & Bretton, Winsford, Manchester Eagles, North Lancs and Stockport.

In Cheshire, Harold 'Jack' Grindley dominated the scene, his list of successes including two wins over Dick Tolley at Birchall Moss Farm, Hatherton on 12 August in a meeting run by the Nantwich & District Motor Club. Indeed, Grindley rode unbeaten at many events, including ones at South Liverpool, Winsford, Rocksavage (Runcorn), Wrexham and a couple at Port Sunlight.

Up in Scotland meetings were run by various organizations, including the East Fife Motorcycle Club, Glasgow Sporting Motorcycle Club at Craigend Castle Grounds, and Dundee & Angus Motor Club at Riverside Park. Among other events, a Scottish Championship was scheduled to take place on 3 September, run by the Craigend Castle Motorcycle Club.

In Ireland, Jack Agnew began his career on the grass and racing was staged at various venues, although the Irish tracks have always had more in common with the rougher terrain-style scrambles circuits. The Dublin & District Motorcycle Club and the Irish Motorcycle Club ran events, with a regular winner being the famous TT rider Stanley Woods.

In Wales there was plenty of action, with the top riders including Dan Thomas, Windy Rees, Ian Williams, Eric Davies, Vic Brinkworth, Herby Jones and Chris Boss. Meanwhile, notable homes for the sport were Carmarthen Park, Cardiff's Sophia Gardens, the Oval at Treorchy (run by the Rhondda Motor Club), the Newbridge circuit at the Recreation Ground, Blaenavon, with race meetings also held in Newport, Aberaman and Pontypool.

Following the opening of St Austell Speedway in 1949, grass-track racing had all but disappeared in the Duchy, but there was some action in the South-West, organized by both the Dartmouth Club and the Otter Vale Club. Top riders in the area were Cecil Macey, Bernard 'Broncho' Slade, Brian Best, John Uglow and Ken Slee.

Regular meetings were run in the Western Centre at Cotheridge (Worcester Auto Club), with the leading local speedsters being Reg Lambourne, Richie Reynolds, Tom Barker and Cornishman Bruce Semmens, who also ran a café in Hereford as well as pursuing a career in speedway!

The South Midland ACU held its regional Championships on 13 August, with the meeting dominated by Jack Colver (Matchless) and Ted Kempson (OK Supreme). The full results were:

> 250cc final – First: Jack Colver, Second: J.P. Driscoll, Third: D. Wilson.
> 350cc final – First: Ted Kempson, Second: Tom Turk, Third: Jimmy Rogers.
> 600cc final – First: Jack Colver, Second: Ted Kempson, Third: Ken Blay.
> Centre Team Shield winners – Wycombe & District Motorcycle Club.

Another major event was the South-East Championships, which were organized by the Surrey Hills Club on 10 September, when Jack Colver was again in winning mood, taking the 250cc title as well as third spot in the 650cc class. The main finals finished thus:

> 250cc final – First: Jack Colver, Second: G.L. Tapp, Third: W. Akers.
> 350cc final – First: Tom Turk, Second: J.F. Cook, Third: Ken Blay.
> 650cc final – First: Dave Spain, Second: Ken Blay, Third: Jack Colver.
> Solo Championship – First: Peter Mould, Second: Arthur Hood, Third:
>   H.J. Donovan.
> Sidecar Championship – First: Don Slate, Second: Les Taylor, Third: H.J. Butler.

Other grass-track meetings during the year took place at Warstock, Redditch and Evesham in the Midlands, whereas the Eastern Centre saw activity through clubs that included Norwich, Grays Tigers and Ilford Amateur.

Sidecar action from an Evesham Club meeting at Netherton, 1950.

MEON VALLEY GRASS TRACK RACES

organised by the

WATERLOOVILLE
MOTOR CYCLE CLUB
Under Permit No. U.252

Garston Farm, East Meon, Hants
(By kind permission of B. M. Cross, Esq.)

16th July, 1950 at 2 p.m.

AN OPEN CENTRE MEETING HELD UNDER THE
GENERAL COMPETITION RULES OF THE AUTO
CYCLE UNION.

OFFICIALS OF THE MEETING :

A.C.U. Steward	C. R. Jones
Club Steward	L. R. Smith
Judges	B. M. Cross, E. Hartridge, F. Weller
Timekeepers	S. Welch, R. Brown
Starter	A. E. Austen
Starters' Marshals	E. Austen, D. Illidge
Lap Scorers	E. Dimmer, A. E. Bryant
Chief Pit Steward	L. Welch
Asst. Pit Marshal	A. H. Simmonds
Machine Examiners	J. Mortlock, R. F. Weller
Treasurer	E. N. L. Guymer
Announcer	A. T. Bull
Clerk of the Course	G. Hodges
Hon. Secretary of the Meeting	A. E. Collins

11th Hants Brigade British Red Cross in attendance

WARNING !

Motor Cycle Racing is dangerous ! You are present at this Meeting entirely at your own risk and subject to the conditions that all persons having any connection with the promotion and/or organisation and/or conduct of the Meeting, including the owners of the land and drivers and owners of the vehicles and passengers in the vehicles are absolved from any liability in respect of personal injury, whether fatal or otherwise, to you, or damage to your property, howsoever caused.

OFFICIAL PROGRAMME - - - - - **SIXPENCE**

Official Programme. **Price 6d.**

UNITED MOTOR CLUB (FROME)
(Affiliated to the Wessex Centre A.C.U.)

This Meeting is Organised under Open to Centre Permit No. M.140, Subject to the General Competition Rules of the A.C.U., including Racing Regulations, Appendix M.

OPEN TO CENTRE GRASS TRACK

RACE MEETING

SUNDAY, JUNE 18th, 1950

AT

THE MOUNT, FROME
(By kind permission of Mr. R. C. Tucker)

First Race, 2.30 p.m.

Officials of the Meeting :

A.C.U. Steward :   Club Steward :
K. RAYMOND, ESQ.   A. RIGG, ESQ.

Official Timekeeper, Handicapper and Judge :
V. ANSTICE, ESQ., A.C.U.

Starter : L. R. SHUTTLEWORTH, ESQ.   Starter's Marshall : J. LEE, ESQ.

Machine Examiner :   Paddock Marshalls :
R. BARNET, ESQ.   E. ARNEY, ESQ.
     A. TURNER, ESQ.

Chief Track Marshal : W. BAKER, ESQ.

Track Marshalls : MEMBERS OF THE UNITED MOTOR CLUB.

Treasurer of the Meeting : R. V. CLACK, ESQ.

Announcer : J. SHELDON, ESQ.

Clerk of the Course : A. D. GREGORY, ESQ.

Secretary of the Meeting : G. H. HODGE, GRAYCOT, LYNFIELD ROAD, FROME.

First Aid by St. John Ambulance Brigade, Frome Division.

Medical Officer of the Meeting : DR. JOHN JAMIESON.

LOUDSPEAKING EQUIPMENT BY ENFIELD'S RADIO SERVICES.

Track : One Quarter of a Mile,

FLAGS : UNION JACK—Start.   CHEQUERED—Finish.   YELLOW—Danger.
     RED—Stop Race.   YELLOW WITH BLACK CROSS—Last Lap.

Spectators are strictly forbidden on the Course and the Organisers do not hold themselves responsible for any accidents.

No Spectators are allowed in the Competitors' Paddock.

THE ELLENBRAY PRESS LTD., FROME.

The Southern Centre enjoyed a full season of racing, with clubs and events including Ringwood at the Mount, Andover, Gosport (Cams Hall), Portsmouth (Southwick), Waterlooville (East Meon), The Ashton Combine (Southampton and Bishop's Waltham Clubs), Blackmore Vale (Tarrant Gunville), Holt, Poole, Sturminster Newton (Dorchester), Salisbury (Laverstock and Amesbury), Bournemouth (Roke Down) and XHG Tigers (Baily Gate, Wimborne). The Centre Championships were held on the Ashton Combine's circuit at Bishop's Waltham, when many top riders participated in the solos, including Stan Lanfear, Jack Vallis, Stan Formhalls, Artie Thick, Lew Coffin, Ross Gilbertson, John Gould, the Lane brothers (Mike and Dave), Bert Croucher, Roy Craighead and Jimmy Squibb. Meanwhile, among others, the sidecar event featured Don Slate, Archie 'Pop' Appleby, Cliff Hazell and Tommy Bounds.

It is certainly interesting to look more closely at some of those who took part in the individual events. Roy Craighead, for example, was passenger to Eric Oliver in a sidecar in the 1930s, and was a regular with Wembley Speedway from 1946 to 1948, prior to representing Southampton, Poole and Norwich. Jimmy Squibb, Jack Vallis and Bert Croucher all rode for Southampton Speedway in the 1950s, while Bert's son, David, was one of the good people responsible for bringing the shale sport back to Wimbledon in 2002. Mike Lane was later to go on and become a Southern Centre sidecar great, while the stories of the legend that is Lew Coffin could fill the pages of an entire book on their own. Ross Gilbertson was to enjoy a long speedway career, during which he rode for several teams, including Aldershot, Southampton, Poole, Romford and Canterbury. Finally, in this brief run through what was only a handful of the entrants from a massive list, the remarkable Stan Formhalls was to ride right up to the year 2000 in vintage events! Rostrum results from the Southern Centre Championships were:

350cc final – First: Bingley Cree (JAP), Second: Stan Formhalls (New Imperial), Third: Lew Coffin (JAP).

Open – First: Bert Croucher (JAP), Second: Dink Philpotts (JAP), Third: Frank Watts (JAP).

Sidecar Championship – First: Archie Appleby (Norton), Second: Don Slate (Norton), Third: Tommy Bounds (BSA).

Looking at the programme for the Waterlooville Motorcycle Club race meeting at Garston Farm, East Meon in Hampshire on 16 July, co-author Dave Stallworthy came across a very interesting name in the list of riders entered. At number twenty-five was a certain R.P. Stallworthy, mounted on a 498cc Scott – this was some eleven years before Dave's brother John transferred from trials to grass-track action, although his 1950 namesake may have possibly been a distant relative from the family tree!

Edgar Fellows, president of the Wessex Centre, gave his review of the season in the *Bristol Evening World* handbook, and began by praising standards at the Highworth Club: 'Reg Wise must be congratulated on the smooth running and efficient way these meetings were run. He installed fencing, and other improvements made accommodation more comfortable. The first meeting was run for the ACU Riders' Benevolent Fund, and Highworth were able to donate £400 [a very large sum in 1950!]. Due to rain though, the Highworth Club finished with a £200 loss from the season's meetings.'

He continued: 'Shepton Mallett also recorded a minus figure (£100), while rain affected the Frome and District and Frome Utd Clubs. Meanwhile, the Farleigh Castle track had a rate assessment that made racing out of the question. Bath had two "wash-outs", and although they were able to raise £200 from a third meeting, overall the club lost £50 over the season. The Stewards would not let the Centre Championships take place as severe weather had made the track unrideable, and the Wessex Centre became £100 out of pocket as well.'

By contrast in the South-East, the Sittingbourne Club's events at the Bull Ground, home of Sittingbourne FC, only suffered one wet meeting out of the four staged on 27 May, 24 June, 22 July and 12 August. At each event the prestigious Silver Helmet was raced for, with Arthur Hood taking two victories, while Sid Jarvis and F. Wood collected one win apiece. These three racers certainly dominated proceedings, with Wood also finishing in second place on two occasions, as well as running a third. Jarvis once ended as runner-up, and filled third spot a couple of times, while double-champion Hood also boasted a second-spot finish.

1950 Roll of Honour

South Midlands Centre Championships
250cc and 600cc – Jack Colver
350cc – Ted Kempson
Team – Wycombe

South-Eastern Centre Championships
250cc – Jack Colver
350cc – Tom Turk
650cc – Dave Spain
Individual – Peter Mould
Sidecar – Don Slate/Reg Nottingham

Southern Centre Championships
350cc – Bingley Cree
Individual – Bert Croucher
Sidecar – Archie Appleby
Club – Southampton

Worcestershire Championship
Len Bayliss

Ashton Combine Championships
Individual – Bert Croucher
Sidecar – Don Slate/Reg Nottingham

Northwich Championship
Bob Parker

Stacey Cup
Ralph Ellison

Farleigh Castle Grand Prix
Bonny Good

Burford Championships
350cc – Reg Lambourne
500cc – Dick Bradley
Sidecar – John Browne

Cardiff Championship
Stan Lanfear

Blackmore Vale Speed Trophy
Bingley Cree and Dink Philpotts (joint-first)

2
GRASS-TRACK RACING
1951

Some wonderful news from 1951 was the first staging of the ACU National Grass-Track Championships, and although the event wasn't held until September it is only right to begin the review of the year with a look at how this panned out. Not only was this billed as the event of the season, it also made history as the National or British Championships have been held every year since. The famous Brands Hatch circuit was written about in *The Story of Grass-track Racing 1927-49*, and it was another well-known venue that was to host the 1951 Nationals – namely Mallory Park. The well-appointed raceway was to go on to stage thousands of motorcycle and car races in the future, and one of the greatest ever battles was witnessed by co-author Dave Stallworthy in 1971, when John 'Moon Eyes' Cooper defeated Italian Giacomo Agostini in the Race of the Year International.

The great day at Mallory Park dawned on Sunday 2 September 1951, when the proceedings entitled as 'An All-England Festival of Britain Grass-track Racing Championship' were organized by the ACU, with assistance from the Leicester Query Motor Club. The circuit measured 1,660 yards in length, and to give some idea of the speeds of the day, Dick Tolley was listed in the programme as the four-lap track-record holder, having clocked 3 minutes 25.4 seconds in July 1951, for an average speed of 67.11mph. The sidecar record, meanwhile, was held by Jack Surtees, who had achieved an average speed of 61.89mph, having been timed at 3 minutes 39.4 seconds in June 1950.

Most of the UK's top riders were in attendance, with the exception of the boys from the South-East, who remained in their own area for the regional Championships, which had been organized for the same day. In the event, however, they could have been at Mallory Park, as the South-Eastern Centre Championships were called off because of rain. The wet stuff also hit Mallory Park on the Saturday, but thankfully the sun shone down on the big day, when estimations of the crowd ranged between 10,000 and 20,000, depending on what report you read!

The Inter-Centre Team Championships were decided on a points basis, with the results being:

Solos – First: East Midlands 43, Second: South Midlands 38, Third: Midlands 36
Sidecars – First: Midlands 34, Second: Southern 30, Third: East Midlands 20

East Midlands aces Fred Wallis and Alf Briggs.

The solo East Midlands side consisted of Syd Mintey (Burdett Special), Fred Wallis (AJS) and Albert Hull (Triumph), while the Midlands sidecar team was made up of Cyril Smith and Bill Boddice, both of whom went on to road-racing fame later in the 1950s. In the individual Championships, Syd Mintey won the 350cc category with ease from a battle royal for second spot featuring Len Bayliss and Naamon Baldwin. Meanwhile there was a close finish in the 500cc class, with Dick Tolley eventually emerging ahead of Fred Wallis and Albert Hull. In the sidecar event, the aforementioned duo of Midlands aces proved to be the drivers going head-to-head for the individual title, and although Bill Boddice appeared to have the race in the bag he drifted wide on the final bend, giving Cyril Smith the historic first Championship. The results summary of the day was:

> 350cc final – First: Syd Mintey (Burdett Special) 3 minutes 53.6 seconds (59.01mph), Second: Len Bayliss (Elbee Special), Third: Naamon Baldwin (BSA).
>
> 500cc final – First: Dick Tolley (Royal Enfield) 3 minutes 43.6 seconds (61.65mph), Second: Fred Wallis (AJS), Third: Albert Hull (Triumph), Fourth: A. Siveyer (AWS).
>
> Sidecar Championship – First: Cyril Smith (Norton) 4 minutes 32.6 seconds (49.36mph), Second: Bill Boddice (Norton), Third: W.W. Mares (Norton).

There was plenty of action across the UK throughout 1951, with venues and clubs including Warton, near Carnforth (North Lancs); Woolgars Farm (Witley); Sywell Aerodrome, Northampton; Eye Park (Diss District & Motorcycle Club); Halwell Cross

(Dartmouth); Lydden Hill (Barham); Woldingham (Carshalton); Stokenchurch (Wycombe); Rocksavage (Runcorn); Folkestone Heights (Folkestone Motorcycle Club); Pontypool Park (Pontypool); Dublin; Treorchy Oval (Rhondda); Welfare Grounds, Newbridge (Pontillanfraith AC); Sophia Gardens (Cardiff); Keighley (Craven District & Motorcycle Club); Mainsforth FC (Ferryhill); Randalls Park (Leatherhead) and Buns Corner (Tenterden).

That was just a selection of the tracks and clubs which held meetings, and looking at a few in more detail, it was interesting to note that the meeting at Warton, organized by the North Lancs Club, also included a Lancashire *v.* Yorkshire team match. With no quarter asked or given, the 'War of the Roses' ended in a victory for Lancashire by 102½ points to 86½.

Racing was still very popular in Wales, with the local club running a meeting at Pontypool Park on Whit Monday afternoon. Close action was the order of the day as Worcester's Richie Reynolds took on the Welsh stars, including Dan Thomas, Gordon Parry and Vic Brinkworth. Meanwhile, the Cardiff Club ran at Sophia Gardens, and in June the UCL Welsh Championships took place. Due to rain, the event had not been held the previous year, and regrettably, although 1949 champion Vic Brinkworth was programmed to ride, he turned out to be a non-starter. Highworth's Roger Wise, of Bristol Speedway fame, went on to lift the Championship Shield following a brilliant display against a classy field, which included another 'cinder-shifter' in Stan Lanfear, who raced for Plymouth and Exeter among others.

At the Pontillanfraith AC event at the Welfare Grounds in Newbridge, Tony Gyselynck and Richie Reynolds were the top riders, while also competing were local aces Roy Zeal and Herby Jones. Another Pontypool meeting was organized in conjunction with the Horticultural Society at Llancayo, when Stan Lanfear, Richie Reynolds and Tony Gyselynck again featured prominently in the results, which were as follows:

350cc final – First: Richie Reynolds, Second: Ted Evans, Third: Ken Wharton.
500cc final – First: Stan Lanfear, Second: Tony Gyselynck, Third: Windy Rees.
Unlimited final – First: Stan Lanfear, Second: Tony Gyselynck, Third: Windy
    Rees.
12-fastest final – First: Stan Lanfear, Second: Tony Gyselynck, Third: Windy Rees.

Clearly South Wales was a good area for grass-track action in this period. Meanwhile, the South-East has always been a popular region for racing, with 1951 being no exception. Four meetings were staged by the Sittingbourne Club at the Bull Ground home of the local football club, each featuring the race for the famous Silver Helmet. Living in the area is keen enthusiast Mick Nokes, who has amazingly recorded every result since the 1920s! For 1951, it was again Arthur Hood taking the coveted trophy on two occasions, while Arthur Fox and Jack Colver each collected one victory. Aside from that, the club also staged the Sittingbourne Championships at the Mall, Faversham in August, with Arthur Hood taking the plaudits for three wins in the 350cc, 500cc and Championship classes, leaving Jack Colver to triumph in the 250cc category. Other clubs to run events in the area were the Leatherhead and District Motorcycle Club (at

Randalls Park), and the Witley Motorcycle Club, both of whom are still very active in organizing modern-day racing.

Further up country in Leicestershire, the Donisthorpe & District Motorcycle and Light Car Club held meetings on a 600-yard semi-mountain-style circuit at West Hill Farm in Appleby Parva. The leading riders at these events included Ralph Ellison, Walter Stanford, Syd Mintey, Len Bayliss, Albert Hull, Denys Goodacre and Austin Cresswell.

Looking at a copy of John and George Gould's events calendar for the year, there was certainly plenty going on in the South. These two riders were to dominate the Southern Centre events throughout the 1950s, and in the season under review they raced at Bere Regis, Newbury, Andover, Overton, Bishop's Waltham, Highworth, Ringwood, Frome, Cannfield, Calne and Pewsey. Emphasizing his prowess in the area, John Gould was victorious in the year's Southern Centre Individual Championship, held at Manor Farm, Brixton Deverill, Warminster.

The West Wilts Club organized just one event at Farleigh Castle, entitled the 'Grand Festival Grass-track'. The meeting included a team race against a side from Kent, while future National Champion Austin Cresswell made his one and only appearance at the famous venue. Unfortunately, the crowd levels had dropped off compared with the golden era of the late 1940s, resulting in a substantial loss for the club of £154.

*Birmingham's Ralph
Ellison speeds
around the track.*

6d. *Official Programme* **6d.**

BLACKMORE VALE M.C.C.
FESTIVAL OF BRITAIN
GRASS TRACK
RACE MEETING
at CANNFIELD, Shaftesbury.

by kind permission of J. YOUNG, Esq.

SUNDAY, 12th AUGUST 1951

Held under A.C.U. Permit No. U.428, and Subject to the General Competition Rules of the A.C.U. including appendix M, the Southern Centre Speed Regulations and the Supplementary Regulations.

OPEN TO THE SOUTHERN CENTRE

Officials of the Meeting :

A.C.U. Centre Steward : G. E. Lemmon
Club Steward : R. E. J. Biddiscombe
Official A. C. U. Timekeeper and Handicapper : A. E. Terry
Clerk of the Course & Secretary of the Meeting : F. J. Rendell
Judges :
P. Farquharson, Esq., J. Young, Esq., S. Bain, Esq., Mrs. S. Bain
Announcer : Capt. Thurston Lewis.
Starter : A. Hollis   *Starters Marshal :* E. L. White
Lap Scorers : J. J. Paul, F. G. Cooper
Machine Examiners : C. C. Burr, A. C. Hickin
Pit Marshalls : H. Savory, J. J. Foot, K. J. Marsh, E. Rideout
Chief Course Marshal : S. Hallett   *Marshals :* Members B.V.M.C.C.
Programmes : Lady Members, B.V.M.C.C.
Gate Marshals : Members British Legion, Shaftesbury Branch,
In charge A. G. Rabbetts
Treasurers of the Meeting : E. S. Drew
First Aid by the Wilts, No.17, British Red Cross
Commandant - E. T. Carter, Esq.

Course 880 yards,   Four Laps to all Heats and Finals

National Champion Dick Tolley again took victory in the Worcestershire Championship, adding to his previous successes of 1946 and 1949, in a meeting run by the Evesham club, the event having been first staged in 1932.

Briefly looking at the racing scene in Ireland, the Easter period is remembered as the time when future Irish Grass-track Champion and international road racer of repute Tommy Robb took the first steps of his illustrious two-wheeled career.

1951 Roll of Honour

National Championships
350cc – Syd Mintey
500cc – Dick Tolley
Sidecar – Cyril Smith/Wilf Willstead
Inter-Centre Team (Solo) – East Midlands
Inter-Centre Team (Sidecar) – Midlands

Southern Centre Championships
125cc – T.J. Sharp
250cc – Triss Sharp
350cc – Dink Philpotts
Individual – John Gould
Sidecar – W. Harris
Team – Bournemouth

South Midlands Centre Championships
125cc – Monty Banks
250cc – Arthur Fox
350cc – Jimmy Rogers
Up to 1000cc – Don Whitebread
Sidecar – Jack Surtees
Team – Grasshopper (Chingford Motorcycle
Club)

North-Western Centre Championship
Naamon Baldwin

East Midlands Centre Championships
Individual – Fred Wallis
Team – Nottingham Tornado

Worcestershire Championship
Dick Tolley

Stainer Trophy
Lew Coffin

Taylor & Chambers Cup
Ralph Ellison

Paul Godfrey Memorial Shield
Dan Thomas

UCL Welsh Championship Shield
Roger Wise

Parsons Novice Championship Shield
W. Doughty

Ashton Solo Championship
Jack Vallis and Dink Philpotts (joint-first)

3
GRASS-TRACK RACING
1952

For 1952, the National Championships moved to Stapleford Tawney Aerodrome in Essex, with the event run by the Ilford Club on behalf of the ACU. An estimated crowd of 4,000 turned out to view the action, and although this probably wasn't as many as expected, it was understandable due to the fact that light rain fell throughout the meeting.

The Inter-Centre Team Championships for sidecar outfits went to the South-East, while the solo version was retained by the Midlands. Meanwhile, Syd Mintey followed up his 1951 success in the 350cc class with a second title ahead of Austin Cresswell, while Fred Wallis eventually filled third spot after getting the better of a tight tussle against Monty Banks and R. Castle. Market gardener Austin Cresswell was victorious in the 500cc final, with Syd Mintey in second position, followed by Ron Pritchard, Eric Burridge and Fred Wallis. Midlander Cresswell had started his career in 1939 at the age of nineteen, and had appeared in just three meetings prior to the outbreak of the Second World War. After a lengthy break he resumed racing in 1948, and his 1952 triumph was to be the first of five National titles for the man who became the grass-track superstar of the 1950s.

The closest race of the day was a three-way dice in the sidecar event between Derek Yorke, Don Slate and Reg Cheney. Going into turn two at a rate of knots, Derek Yorke made a mistake and suffered an exclusion for leaving the track, with race victory finally going to Don Slate on board his Norton outfit. The finals resulted thus:

> 350cc final – First: Syd Mintey (Burdett Special), Second: Austin Cresswell (Enfield JAP), Third: Fred Wallis (AJS), Fourth: Monty Banks (BSA).
> 500cc final – First: Austin Cresswell (Enfield JAP), Second: Syd Mintey (Burdett Special), Third: Fred Wallis (AJS), Fourth: Eric Burridge (JAP).
> Sidecar Championship – First: Don Slate (Norton), Second: R. Cheney (Norton JAP), Third: Ted Furniss (AJS JAP).

Reserve races were also staged, and just for the record the recorded results were:

> 350cc – First: Slant Payling, Second: Lew Coffin, Third: G. Sporles.
> 500cc – First: Tony Swift, Second: Arthur Hood, Third: George Gould.
> Sidecar – First: Harold Hill, Second: J. Thorn, Third: G.W. Pretty.

Racing was still taking place at Mallory Park, the scene of the previous year's National Championships. Syd Mintey was the top speedster in the 350cc class at the venue, while 1951 champion Dick Tolley was the man to beat in the 500s. Other leading riders to appear at the famous raceway during the year included Tony Gyselynck, Eric Burridge, Jim Tolley, Peter Hall, Eddie Blackwell, Vic Holcroft, Fred Wallis and Ken Greer in the solos, while the sidecar events featured Charlie Freeman, Alf Ellis, Sid Hall and Tommy Westwood.

The North-Western Centre Champion was Naamon Baldwin, who was at one time a director of Fleetwood Speedway, as well as being a friend of the popular ukulele player and entertainer George Formby. Naamon was quite a character, as he raced a gold-painted JAP, and wore matching leathers, entering his steed at race meetings as the 'Golden Eagle'.

A series of events were again organized by the Sittingbourne Club in the South-East sector, where Jack Colver, Arthur Fox and Tom Albery became Silver Helmet winners. Albery was a versatile rider, with a keen interest in grass-track's sister sport, being a competitor at California Speedway. He was to go on and become a founder member of the Southern Centre Grass-track Riders' Association, as well as appearing in vintage events in the 1970s. Ken Smith was victorious in the Sittingbourne Championship at the Mall, Faversham, while Sid Jarvis defeated Monty Banks and Peter Mould to lift the South-Eastern Individual Championship at the Eltham's Valley circuit.

Racing in the South and West took place at Shepton Mallet (Doulting), Ashton Keynes (Shorncote), Reading (Bath Road), Broadhembury (Willand), Gosport, Marlborough, Farleigh Castle, Devizes (Swan Meadow), Feniton, Ringwood (the Mount) and Newquay. The Otter Vale Motor Club organized the action at Chelsea Farm, Feniton in Devon, and Lew Coffin was the star of the first meeting at the venue, winning three of the finals, although he came second to Adrian Kessell in the 8-Fastest final. Other notable riders in the solos-only event were Cecil Macey, the Gould brothers (John and George), Herbie Plain and Jack (also known as John) Uglow, while just beginning his career was Henry Body, mounted on Velocette (250cc) and Triumph (500cc) machinery.

A name that later went down as something special in the history of grass-track racing was the Minety Vale Club. They organized meetings at Shorncote, near Ashton Keynes in Gloucestershire. To start with, Minety Vale received help from Cirencester Motorcycle Club and Swindon & District Motorcycle Club, with much equipment loaned to them by the Highworth Motorcycle & Light Car Club. Their first meeting took place on 1 June, using a 600-yard racetrack, with the results being:

> Clubmans Unlimited final – First: Austin Cresswell, Second: Jim Webb,
>   Third: Artie Thick.
> First Unlimited final – First: Dink Philpotts, Second: John Gould, Third: Austin
>   Cresswell.
> Second Unlimited final – First: John Gould, Second: George Gould,
>   Third: Austin Cresswell.
> Sidecar final – First: Don Slate, Second: A. Spencer.
> Sidecar Handicap final – First: Cliff Hazell, Second: Don Slate.

Mentioned in the previous volume, covering 1927-1949, was the fact that grass-track racing had taken place at Alton Towers, and the Staffordshire venue again saw race action in July 1952, with the staging of the ACU National Rally Grass-track. Moving a little further up country, Cheshire was also a hotbed for racing via the Nantwich Club, who ran the show locally at Birchall Moss Farm, Hatherton.

Other notable venues that saw action during the year included Hopwell Park, Risley, near Long Eaton; Wrottesley Park, Wolverhampton and Randalls Park, Leatherhead.

On 27 July, the Ringwood Club ran a meeting at the Mount, a famous venue that first hosted racing way back in 1927. Bryan Sharp, Brian Hannam, John Gould, Dave Lane and Lew Coffin all won a final apiece, and later in the year John Gould returned to lift the Southern Centre Individual Championship.

The Broadhembury Club's event took place at Lower Coombe, Willand, Cullompton on 7 September, with the main event being an Open Championship, which was won by Exeter Speedway rider Vic Gent, ahead of Jack Light and Herbie Plain. The 500cc title also went the way of Vic Gent, while Adrian Kessell defeated future sidecar champion Mike Lane in the 350cc class, leaving Broncho Slade to claim victory in the 8-Fastest final. Remarkably, the village of Willand was to see top class grass-track racing fifty years on, with the staging of the 2002 British Best Pairs event.

At Farleigh Castle just one meeting was staged on 14 September, when the Enfield Club joined forces with Frome Utd. John Gould emerged victorious in the Rob Walker Challenge Trophy, while 1951 National Champion Dick Tolley made his first visit to the renowned circuit.

Famous speedway and grass-track author Cyril May was behind a one-off Wessex Centre meeting on 20 September, when Devizes & District Motor Club had 4,000 spectators turn up to watch the grass gladiators go through their paces at Swan Meadow, Pewsey in Wiltshire.

OFFICIAL PROGRAMME

DEVIZES and DISTRICT MOTOR CLUB

Presents

MOTOR CYCLE GRASS TRACK RACING

at

SWAN MEADOW, PEWSEY, WILTS

(By kind permission of Mrs. S. A. Rawlins)

on

SATURDAY, SEPTEMBER 20th, at 2.30 p.m.

(for the Pewsey Carnival Committee)

DICK BRADLEY in action   Photo.   C. M

1952 Roll of Honour

National Championships
350cc – Syd Mintey
500cc – Austin Cresswell
Sidecar – Don Slate/Reg Nottingham
Inter-Centre Team (Solo) – East Midlands
Inter-Centre Team (Sidecar) – South-East

Southern Centre Championships
120cc – Triss Sharp
250cc – Bryan Sharp
350cc – Dink Philpotts
Individual – John Gould
Team – Bournemouth

South Midlands Centre Championships
125cc – Ernie Watson
250cc – Arthur Fox
350cc – Eric Burridge
Up to 1,000cc – Alf Hagon
Team – Grasshopper (Chingford Motorcycle Club)

North-Western Centre Championship
Naamon Baldwin

Worcestershire Championship
Len Bayliss

Stainer Trophy
Lew Coffin

UCL Welsh Championship Shield
Tony Gyselynck

Cheshire Centre Championship
Ralph Ellison

Eric Fernihough Trophy
Lew Coffin

East Yorkshire Championship
Jack Adams

Rob Walker Challenge Trophy
John Gould

Minety Vale Championships
350cc – Bill Hopkins
Unlimited – Ken Wiggins
Junior – Artie Harwood
Sidecar – F.R. Lewis

Minety Vale Shorncote Championships
Solo – Len Bayliss
Sidecar – Reg Lewis

Eastern Centre Championships
125cc – W.G. Brister
200cc – T. Warren
250cc – R. Henderson
350cc – A. Hooper
500cc – Jack Hubbard
Sidecar – Derek Yorke

Midland Centre Championship
Ron Pritchard

South-Eastern Centre Championships
250cc – Arthur Fox
350cc – Jack Colver
650cc – Dave Spain snr
Solo – Sid Jarvis
Sidecar – Don Slate/Reg Nottingham

Broadhembury Open Championship
Vic Gent

4
GRASS-TRACK RACING
1953

It was estimated that 12,000 spectators turned out to watch the third staging of the National Grass-track Championships. Held amid warm and dry weather, the prestigious event was back at Mallory Park in Leicestershire. The line-up was again an impressive array of oval-track talent, with the solo competitors featuring Dick Tolley (500cc Champion in 1951), Austin Cresswell (500cc Champion in 1952) and Syd Mintey (350cc Champion in both 1951 and 1952).

Aside from the previous victors, the list also included Alf Hagon, who went on to become a real legend in the sport, plus Midlands ace Len Bayliss, scrambles star Phil Nex, and South-Eastern racers Martin 'Spud' Tatum and Jack Colver. Then there were 'Welsh Wizards' Roy Zeal and Dan Thomas, with the South Midlands area represented by Monty Banks and Jimmy Rogers. The top names just went on and on, with Southern Centre Champion John Gould also competing, as well as former Southampton Speedway rider Cecil Bailey, who later went on to be a renowned motorcycle photographer. Meanwhile in the sidecars, both previous victors, Cyril Smith (1951) and Don Slate (1952), were unfortunately not present, meaning there would be a new Champion, with the leading protagonists being Derek Yorke, Bill Evans, Ted Davis, Harold Hill, Charlie Freeman, Hilton Woodrow, Eddie Summers and Freddie French.

The track was 1,660 yards in length, which was certainly large compared with the present day. The riders weren't hanging about, however, as emphasized when Austin Cresswell recorded an average speed of 70.05mph! Bearing in mind that was fifty years ago, it shows just how quickly the top boys were going on the big oval circuit.

In the 350cc Championship, Syd Mintey again scooped first place to complete a wonderful hat-trick of titles, leading all the way from start to finish, with Austin Cresswell doing likewise to retain his 500cc crown. The sidecar final proved to be the most exciting event, with Bill Evans initially leading on his Norton, only to go out after being hit by mechanical problems. That left Derek Yorke and Ted Davis to do battle, and following a great tussle, it was Yorke who just got home ahead by half a wheel!

The Inter-Centre Team Championships resulted in a third successive triumph for the East Midlands in the solo class, while the Midlands took the sidecar honours. The main finals of the big event resulted thus:

350cc final – First: Syd Mintey (Burdett Special), Second: Fred Wallis (AJS JAP), Third: Alf Hagon (BSA JAP), Fourth: Austin Cresswell (Enfield JAP).

500cc final – First: Austin Cresswell (Enfield JAP), Second: Len Bayliss (Elbee Special), Third: Dick Tolley (Enfield JAP), Fourth: Syd Mintey (Burdett Special).

Sidecar Championship – First: Derek Yorke (Rudge JAP), Second: Ted Davis (Vincent), Third: Charlie Freeman (Norton), Fourth: Freddie French (JAP).

Although they might not have been successful in the National Championships, several of those present went on to lift other titles in 1953. For example, John Gould was to again emerge victorious in the 500cc category at the Southern Centre Championships, while Dick Tolley reigned supreme in the prestigious Worcestershire Championship. Monty Banks blazed to glory in the South Midlands Championships, taking the chequered flag in no less than four events, namely 200cc, 250cc, 350cc and 500cc! Alf Hagon took victory in the South-Eastern Centre Championships, while Len Bayliss followed suit in the Midlands Centre. By the same token, in the sidecars, major titles went the way of Mike Lane (Southern Centre), Freddie French (South Midlands) and Hilton Woodrow (South-East).

At the Sittingbourne Club's Wrinsted Court circuit, Sid Jarvis (twice), Jack Colver and Martin Tatum took the accolades in the coveted Silver Helmet events, while the Eltham Club also successfully organized racing at the Valley in Frinsted.

Down in the South-West, racing took place at Chiverton Cross, Blackwater in the Duchy of Cornwall, run by the Camborne & Redruth Motorcycle and Light Car Club. Meanwhile, a little further up country, Shuttleton Farm in Hemyock played host to some fast and furious action, organized by the Broadhembury & District Motor Club. The Cornish event was of a scrambles nature, but included among the competitors was one Adrian Kessell, who was later to go on and win the South-Western Centre Championship. At Hemyock, 'Kess' was to win the 350cc, 500cc and 8-Fastest finals, although he did take a rare fall in the Unlimited category. Still, three victories was a great achievement, as the meeting featured a talented field, with the top riders including Lew Coffin, Vic Gent, Dink Philpotts, Ken Slee, Cecil Macey, Brian Best, Herbie Plain, Garth Jotcham, Jack Uglow and the Gould brothers.

Another West Country grass-track was the West of England Motor Club's circuit, situated at the Showground, Whipton in Exeter. They ran on Saturday evenings, and winners at the venue included Adrian Kessell and Cecil Macey, with other top-notch competitors including Vic Gent, Broncho Slade, Lew Coffin and Wally Monckton.

The Enfield Club were now running at Farleigh Castle, south of Bath, with John Gould taking victory in the Enfield Challenge Trophy. In all, three events were held at the venue, with the largest crowd of some 3,250 attending the first staged.

The Minety Vale Club were again running at Shorncote, Ashton Keynes; the Ringwood Club in the South were still based at the Mount; the Blackmore Vale Club established the famous Willoughby Hedge venue; Shepton Mallet had moved from Doulting to Rodmore Park. Meanwhile, another grass venue which would go on to great acclaim was the Evesham Club's circuit at Ham Dean Farm, Pinvin, near Pershore in Worcestershire.

The Minety Vale events at Shorncote always attracted an all-star line-up to race on a 500-yard circuit. Dick Tolley clocked a track record of 86.6 seconds at the venue during the year, and was also victorious in the 350cc Club Championship in their last meeting of the season on 13 September, when he defeated George Gould and Len Bayliss in the final. Meanwhile, R. Griffiths from Wales emerged as the Junior Champion from the event, with the field including several riders who were to progress in the sport, most notably Peter Hall, Glyn Chandler, Doug Drewett and local rider Mike Keen. Of course, both Keen and Chandler were also to take up careers on shale, enjoying varying degrees of success with Swindon, although the latter also had spells with Neath, Cradley Heath, Oxford and Long Eaton. The Unlimited Championship went to Hereford's Ray Harris, who was another rider to enjoy a stint for Swindon Speedway, although for much of his career he was identified with Stoke. The full results of the Unlimited Championship were:

Heat one – First: Adrian Kessell, Second: Dave Lane, Third: Dave Main.
Heat two – First: Ray Harris, Second: George Gould, Third: D. Collins.
Heat three – First: Ray Beaumont, Second: Richie Reynolds, Third: J. Brown.
Heat four – First: Len Bayliss, Second: Artie Harwood, Third: Malcolm Snook.
Heat five – First: John Gould, Second: Lew Coffin, Third: W.J. Legg.
First Semi-final – First: Ray Harris, Second: John Gould, Third: Adrian Kessell.
Second Semi-final – First: Len Bayliss, Second: Lew Coffin, Third: George Gould.
Final – First: Ray Harris, Second: Len Bayliss, Third: John Gould.

Harking back to the Blackmore Vale Club's new circuit, the initial meeting was held on 19 July, and later in the year they ran the first Willoughby Hedge Championships on Sunday 20 September. The top prize money was awarded for the 500cc solo and sidecar events, with the winners able to claim the princely sum of £5 on top of their trophies. 'Mr Blackmore Vale' Jim Rendell was the secretary for the meeting, as indeed he was for many years at the club's race events. Southern Centre Champion John Gould proved to be in fine form, taking victory in the 350cc, 500cc and Up to 1,000cc finals, while Fred Parkins from Parkstone, near Poole, won both the Novice final and the Experts Barred event. The £7 in prize money that Fred received for his two successes would, incidentally, have been equal to a week's wages, or more, in 1953. In the sidecars, Birmingham's John Lidgate, mounted on his 500cc Ariel JAP took victory, with Eddie Summers crossing the line first in the handicapped event. Other top solo riders listed in the programme who didn't feature in the results included Adrian Kessell, Cecil Macey, Jack Vallis, Ray Beaumont and Dink Philpotts, while other leading sidecar entrants were Jack Difazio, Ray Gerring and Cliff Hazell. Results from the Willoughby Hedge Championships follow:

350cc final – First: John Gould, Second: Lew Coffin, Third: A. Read.
500cc final – First: John Gould, Second: Roy Goulding, Third: Eddie Blackwell.
Up to 1,000cc final – First: John Gould, Second: Dick Tolley, Third: George Gould.

Experts Barred final – First: Fred Parkins, Second: J. Coughlan, Third: Pat
   Waterman.

Novice final – First: Fred Parkins, Second: Wally Monckton, Third: T. Cattle.

Sidecar final – First: John Lidgate, Second: Eddie Summers, Third: Tommy
   Bounds.

Sidecar Handicap final – First: Eddie Summers, Second: Tommy Bounds,
   Third: Mike Lane.

Clubs active in Cheshire and the North-West were Runcorn at Rocksavage; North Lancs at Warton; Westmorland at Helsington; Wigan & St Helens AC at Wrightington; and Nantwich at George's Playing Fields. Meanwhile the Winsford Club organized the Centre Championships, which saw Austin Cresswell win narrowly from Manchester-born speedway man Bert Lacey. The Moccasin Club (Prestwich) held the North-Western Centre Championships at Hopwood in Lancashire, where the aforementioned Lacey took the title from Maurice 'Tuner' Wilkinson of Kettlewell, North Yorkshire in a real 'War of the Roses'. Other notable riders in the region during the year included Ralph Ellison, Jack Grindley, Eric Pickup, Andy Courtney, Harry Terretta and Bill Bridgett.

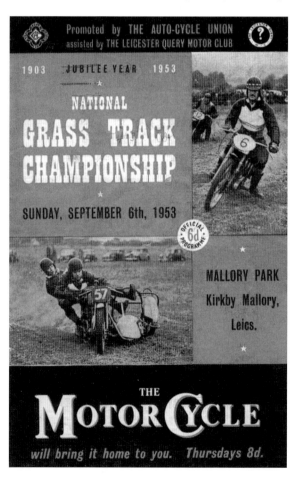

In Northern Ireland, future motorcycle legend Sammy Miller was victorious in the 200cc Ulster Championship, and for good measure the year also saw him triumph in the 200cc Ulster Sand Racing Championship. Later he became a top road-racer, and in 1957 he finished third in the 250cc World Championship, but it was trials riding at which he excelled, winning the British title on eleven occasions, as well as twice becoming European Champion (the forerunner of the World Championship).

1953 Roll of Honour

National Championships
350cc – Syd Mintey
500cc – Austin Cresswell
Sidecar – Derek Yorke/George Mason
Inter-Centre Team (Solo) – East Midlands
Inter-Centre Team (Sidecar) – Midlands

Southern Centre Championships
250cc – Triss Sharp
350cc – Lew Coffin
Individual – John Gould
Sidecar – Mike Lane/Bill Woodward
Team – Bournemouth

South Midlands Centre Championships
125cc – Peter Taft
200cc, 250cc, 350cc and 500cc – Monty Banks
Sidecar – Freddie French/George Wasley
Team – Grasshopper (Chingford MC)

North-Western Centre Championship
Bert Lacey

Cheshire Centre Championship
Austin Cresswell

Worcestershire Championship
Dick Tolley

Minety Vale Championships
350cc – Dick Tolley
Unlimited – Ray Harris
Junior – R. Griffiths
Sidecar – Dave Dutton/G. Hall

Minety Vale Riders' Championship
Dick Tolley

Midland Centre Championship
Len Bayliss

South-Eastern Centre Championships
250cc and 350cc – L.W. 'Buster' Brown
Solo and 650cc – Alf Hagon
Sidecar – Hilton Woodrow

South-Western Centre Championship
Adrian Kessell

Blackmore Vale Speed Trophy
George Gould

Carnival Kings 350cc Cup
Austin Cresswell

Farleigh Castle Championships
1,000cc – John Gould
Junior – Peter Hall
Sidecar – John Browne

Enfield Challenge Trophy
John Gould

Cambridgeshire Championship
Lightweight – Vic Bright
Junior and Senior – Austin Cresswell

Willoughby Hedge Championships
350cc and 500cc – John Gould
Junior – Fred Parkins
Sidecar – John Lidgate

Richmond Trophy
Paul Pritchard

Irish Five-Mile Championship
Ernie Lyons

Ulster 200cc Championship
Sammy Miller

5
GRASS-TRACK RACING
1954

The National Championships were again staged at Mallory Park, for the third time in the four-year history of the event. There was a new name taking the honours, however, as Alf Hagon from the Eastern Centre burst to the fore. The first signs that Syd Mintey would be up against it in his quest for a fourth title came in the 350cc team races. These saw Hagon speed to victory over Austin Cresswell and Martin Tatum, while Mintey could only run a second behind Yorkshire's R. Lawrence. Then, in the first heat of the 500cc team races, Hagon dashed to the flag from Cresswell and John Gould, setting a new track record of 70.98mph in the process.

In the 350cc Individual Championship, both Syd Mintey and Alf Hagon took victory in their respective heats, so it was showdown time in the final. Hagon duly hit the front on his BSA, and held that position to lift his first national title. However, he was really made to work for it, as Mintey stayed on his back wheel all the way, providing the crowd with plenty of excitement. In a repeat performance, Hagon again held off Mintey in the 500cc final to complete a fabulous double, but he had to move pretty quickly to stay ahead, establishing an even quicker track record of 71.35mph.

The sidecar event was dominated by the Norton-mounted Bill Evans, who defeated 1953 title-winner Derek Yorke in the team race, prior to beating Charlie Freeman in his Championship heat. Yorke also took the chequered flag in his heat and in a faster time too, but it was to be Evans' year as he swept home in the final with ease, thereby making up for the disappointment of his mechanical failure of the previous year. Freddie French, who had won his first major title in the 1953 South Midlands Centre Championships, filled the runner-up position, while Yorke went out with a flat tyre. The results from the main finals were recorded thus:

> 350cc final – First: Alf Hagon (BSA), Second: Syd Mintey (Burdett Special),
>   Third: Martin Tatum (AJS), Fourth: Austin Cresswell (Enfield JAP).
> 500cc final – First: Alf Hagon (BSA), Second: Syd Mintey (Burdett Special),
>   Third: Martin Tatum (AJS), Fourth: John Gould (JAP).
> Sidecar Championship – First: Bill Evans (Norton), Second: Freddie French
>   (Norton JAP), Third: H.E. Carter (Norton JAP).

Syd Mintey (25) leads from Arthur Stuffins (2) on a tight inside line.

The National Team Championships went to the Midlands in both the solo and sidecar classes, leaving the day belonging to Alf Hagon and Bill Evans. Finally, in this brief look at the Nationals, a glance at the programme gives a good indication of the all-star field on show, which included Lew Coffin, Len Bayliss, George Gould, Eddie Blackwell, Fred Wallis, Alf Goodey, Jimmy Rogers, Monty Banks, Arthur Stuffins and scrambler Brian Stonebridge in the solos. Meanwhile, the sidecar line-up featured Vic Artus, Hilton Woodrow and Fred Pusey from Cheshire, the father of future solo British Champion Chris.

So to some of the ACU regional Championships of the year, and it was Hampshire's John Gould who retained his 500cc individual crown in the Southern Centre, with the event held at the Blackmore Vale Club's Willoughby Hedge circuit. In defeating Midlander John Lidgate, the meeting also saw Mike Lane hold on to his sidecar title, while the team event was scooped by Blackmore Vale, who used home turf to maximum advantage. The finals resulted thus:

125cc final – First: P.J. Horner, Second: T. Stephens, Third: C. Exstance.
350cc final – First: Eddie Blackwell, Second: George Gould, Third: Lew Coffin.
500cc final – First: John Gould, Second: Eddie Blackwell, Third: Ray Beaumont.
Sidecar final – First: Mike Lane, Second: John Lidgate, Third: A. Spencer.

Over in the South Midlands, Austin Cresswell was victorious in the Up to 1,000cc category, while top scrambler Andy Lee carried off the 350cc title. Andy was, of course, the father of 1981 World Long-track Champion Michael Lee, who also won the World

Super action as Austin Cresswell (200) heads Arthur Stuffins.

Speedway final the year before at the Ullevi Stadium, Gothenburg in Sweden. The Centre Championships were organized by the Roosters Club and held at Sherington, near Newport Pagnell, a venue also used by the North Bucks Club. A large crowd, estimated at around 4,000, watched the action, which also saw sidecar ace Freddie French retain the title he had claimed in 1953. Results from the prestigious meeting follow:

> 125cc final – First: Paul Taft (BSA), Second: T. Connor (BSA), Third: C. Adams (BSA).
> 200cc final – First: Ernie Watson (DOT), Second: Andy Lee (Francis Barnett), Third: Ted Ryman (Francis Barnett).
> 250cc final – First: Peter Taft (BSA), Second: P. Mitchell (Ariel), Third: R. Slade (JAP).
> 350cc final – First: Andy Lee (Francis Barnett), Second: Austin Cresswell (Royal Enfield), Third: Ernie Watson (JAP).
> Up to 1,000cc final – First: Austin Cresswell (Royal Enfield), Second: Alf Hagon (BSA), Third: Martin Tatum (Royal Enfield-JAP).
> Sidecar final – First: Freddie French (Norton JAP), Second: Brian Stonebridge (BSA), Third: Eric Smeed (Norton JAP).

It was certainly a gathering of the stars, for along with Andy Lee, the Taft brothers and Brian Stonebridge were leading scramblers of the day, while Austin Cresswell, Alf Hagon and Martin Tatum were all set for a long time at the cutting edge of the grass-track world.

Aside from Sherington, other race meetings that took place in the South Midlands area were staged at Wingrove, Burnham Beeches, organized by the Farnham Royal Club, and at Eaton Bray, Dunstable, run by the Slough and Luton Club.

Further east, the Castle Colchester Club hosted the Eastern Centre Championships at Westhouse Farm, Lexdon, with a large crowd of some 5,000 in attendance. By filling third place in the 200cc class another scrambler featured prominently in the results, namely the great Dave Bickers, who later became European Scrambles Champion, and winner of the BBC Grandstand series. Alf Hagon and Alf Goodey came out on top of the Up to 1,000cc and 350cc Championships respectively, while H.E. Carter grabbed the sidecar title. The main finals resulted thus:

> 200cc final – First: Tony Sutton (Francis Barnett), Second: Monty Banks (Tandon), Third: Dave Bickers (DOT).
> 250cc final – First: D. Slaughter (Triumph), Second: F. Warnell (DOT), Third: A. Ratcliffe (Velocette).
> 350cc final – First: Alf Goodey (JAP), Second: Ernie Watson (JAP), Third: Alf Hagon (BSA).
> Up to 1,000cc final – First: Alf Hagon (BSA JAP), Second: Jack Hubbard (Matchless), Third: Monty Banks (BSA).
> Sidecar final – First: H.E. Carter (Norton JAP), Second: Eric Smeed (Norton JAP), Third: Derek Yorke (Rudge JAP).

Support races for the meeting resulted as follows:

> Junior – First: E.J. Bass (JAP), Second: C.C. Webb (JAP), Third: W.J. Calver (Ariel).
> Senior – First: Alf Hagon (BSA), Second: Alf Goodey (JAP), Third: Ernie Watson (JAP).
> Sidecar Handicap – First: Eric Smeed (Norton JAP), Second: H.R. Moore (Ariel), Third: H.E. Carter (Norton JAP).

Not to be outdone, the Northern Centre held their Championships at Calder Bridge in Cumbria, organized by the Whitehaven Club, with the winners being F. Hetherington (250cc), Billy Milburn (350cc), and Angus Tyson (351 to 1,000cc).

It wasn't just about titles, for there was action all over the UK for novices and experts alike, with a general cross-section of the venues including Quibell Park, Scunthorpe, Lincolnshire; White Way Hill, Exton, Hampshire (The Ashton Combine); Gainsborough, Lincolnshire (Derby Phoenix Club); Birchall Moss Farm, Hatherton, Nantwich, Cheshire; Old Cricket Ground, Warrington Road, Runcorn, Cheshire; Manor Farm, Fremington, Devon; Middlemoor, Countess Wear, Exeter, Devon (Broadhembury Club); Moor Farm, Coleorton, Ashby-de-la-Zouch, Leicestershire; Lydden Hill, near Folkestone, Kent (Barham Club); Bampton Road, Tiverton, Devon; Dog Hill Farm, Dormansland, East Grinstead, Sussex; Bentons Farm, Stanford-le-Hope, Essex; Wye Valley, Woolhope, near Hereford; Bidford-on-Avon, Warwickshire (Evesham Club);

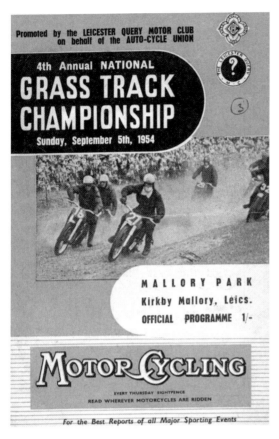

Reg Lambourne (1) leads the way at the Ledbury Floral Fete, 1954.

St Ann's chapel, Bigbury, near Dartmouth, Devon; Middle Barn Farm, Pulborough, West Sussex; Allsops Lane, Loughborough, Leicestershire; Skinners Farm, Abridge, Essex; Wrottesley Park, Wolverhampton and Manor Farm, Shapwick, near Bridgwater, Somerset.

In the Wessex Centre it was out with the old and in with the new as the Enfield No. 2 Works Club ran what turned out to be the final three grass-track events at Farleigh Castle, until a one-off meeting was held at the famous venue in 1991. The podium positions at the last meeting of 1954 were filled by John Gould from Bill Bridgett and Malcolm Snook in the Farleigh Castle Grand Prix, with the same two men occupying first and second places in the Enfield Challenge Trophy, ahead of Len Bayliss.

It might have been goodbye to Farleigh Castle, but it was hello to Long Newnton, as the Minety Vale Club began running meetings from a new track situated at the airfield on the Malmesbury to Tetbury road. The meetings at Long Newnton were to prove popular, and over the eight years that followed the venue became just about as famous as any of the major circuits within the sport. The racing strip was oval-shaped, being 650 yards in length, and the top meeting of the year was for the Long Newnton Championships on 26 September. Hereford's Ray Harris was to win the event, finishing ahead of Adrian Kessell, Artie Harwood and Welshman R. Griffiths.

Another renowned track, which was to have a longer lifespan than that of Long Newnton, was the one at Ham Dean Farm, Pinvin. The Evesham Club ran their annual meeting at the Worcestershire venue on 11 July, and prior to that, the equally famous Mount circuit at Ringwood echoed to the sound of racing on 27 June.

A brief look at the Sittingbourne & Eltham Club's race meetings, staged at both Wrinsted Court and the Valley, Frinsted, revealed two Silver Helmet triumphs for Martin Tatum, plus one apiece for Jack Colver and Arthur Hood. Meanwhile, 'Spud' Tatum was successful in the Redshaw Trophy on 12 September in a meeting that also featured Alf Hagon. Other top solo riders to race at the Sittingbourne events over the year included Monty Banks, Arne Hendriksen, Pete Mitchell and Pat Sims, while Hilton Woodrow, Freddie French and Bert Brett represented the sidecar fraternity.

Ernie Lyons, riding a Triumph JAP, won the Irish Five-Mile Championship, with Tommy Robb sprinting to success in the 350cc category. This event took place at a Butlin's holiday camp in County Meath, Eire. Elsewhere, the Bray & District Motorcycle Club ran their very first meeting at the Earl of Meath's estate near Bray on Sunday 16 May, when the race winners included Ernie Callaghan, Mervyn Hayes and Harry Lindsay. In a conversation with co-author Dave Stallworthy, Irish speedster Jack Agnew recalled that the machines used in Ireland were more like roadsters. He also recalled racing against top-class men like Tony McCleary, Noel Bell, Bertie Mann and Leslie Wright in the North, while down in the south of the country the leading lights were Mervyn Hayes, Doug Pearson, Gerry Scarlett and the Williams brothers, Eric and Ian.

1954 Roll of Honour

National Championships
350cc and 500cc – Alf Hagon
Sidecar – Bill Evans/Ron Jones
Inter-Centre Team (Solo) – Midlands
Inter-Centre Team (Sidecar) - Midlands

Southern Centre Championships
125cc – P.J. Horner
350cc – Eddie Blackwell
Individual – John Gould
Sidecar – Mike Lane/Bill Woodward
Team – Blackmore Vale

South Midlands Centre Championships
125cc – Paul Taft
200cc – Ernie Watson
250cc – Peter Taft
350cc – Andy Lee
1,000cc – Austin Cresswell
Sidecar – Freddie French/George Wasley
Team – Grasshopper (Chingford
Motorcycle Club)

Cheshire Centre Championships
200cc – J. Sellers
350cc – Bert Lacey
500cc and Clubmans – Bill Bridgett
Unlimited – Eric Pope

Eastern Centre Championships
200cc – Tony Sutton
250cc – D. Slaughter
350cc – Alf Goodey
1,000cc – Alf Hagon
Sidecar – H.E. Carter

Northern Centre Championships
250cc – F. Hetherington
350cc – Billy Milburn
1,000cc – Angus Tyson

East Midlands Centre Championship
Austin Cresswell

East Midlands Team Championship
Loughborough Motorcycle Club

Worcestershire Championship
Austin Cresswell

James Mintey Memorial Trophy
(Experts Barred)
Peter Hall

Long Newnton Championships
350cc – Lew Coffin
Unlimited – Ray Harris

Long Newnton Laurels
John Gould

Fordham Handicap Trophy
Monty Banks

Ledbury Garden Fete Trophy
Bill Bridgett

Eric Fernihough Trophy
Lew Coffin

Carnival Kings Sidecar Cup
Fred Hanks

Farleigh Castle Grand Prix
John Gould

Enfield Challenge Trophy
John Gould

Cambridgeshire Championship
Austin Cresswell

Irish Five Ride Championship
350cc – Tommy Robb
500cc – Ernie Lyons

6
GRASS-TRACK RACING
1955

There was a new venue for the National Championships in this year, namely Sywell Aerodrome, near Northampton, in the South Midlands ACU area. On a 1,000 yard circuit, the event was promoted by the Beds, Herts & Northants Trials group on behalf of the ACU. In what turned out to be a rather dusty meeting, the solo Inter-Centre Team Championship was won by the Midlands, ahead of the East Midlands, with the Southern Centre in third position. In the sidecars, something of a reverse situation resulted, with the East Midlands leading home the Midlands and the Eastern Centre. Austin Cresswell, Syd Mintey, Dave Nourish and Ralph Ellison took victories in the 350cc team races, while in the 500s, there was a win apiece for brothers John and George Gould, plus one

John Warren (74), pictured at the National Championships, 1955.

for Lew Coffin. Also taking the chequered flag in the 500cc event was Ralph Ellison, who thereby completed a wonderful double. Meanwhile, there were sidecar successes for Freddie French, Harold Hill and John Warren.

The individual Championships brought two new title victors, the 350cc category going to Triumph JAP-mounted Denys Goodacre, who incidentally appears on the front cover of this publication. The 500cc winner, meanwhile, turned out to be Martin Tatum, the father of Kelvin, who of course later became British Speedway Champion in both 1987 and 1990, as well as a triple World Long-track Champion (1995, 1998 and 2000). In the sidecars, the crown again went to Bill Evans, ahead of his friend and on-track rival Harold Hill. The hard-luck story of the day surely belonged to southerner George Gould in the 500cc class, as he won both his team race and Championship heat, only to retire from the final with mechanical problems. Syd Mintey, meanwhile, was still taking top placings in the Nationals, with a sixth-place finish in the 500cc event behind Tatum, Len Bayliss, Wally Monckton, Maurice Wilkinson (father of Bill and Mick, who later became top trials riders) and Goodacre.

It is possible that a mistake occurred in the results from the 500cc event, as Wally Monckton appeared to have caught up to snatch the runner-up spot on the line. However, the following is how the official results were recorded:

> 350cc final – First: Denys Goodacre (Triumph JAP), Second: Arne Hendriksen (JAP), Third: Austin Cresswell (Royal Enfield JAP), Fourth: Stan Bassett (Begrie Special), Fifth: Martin Tatum (JAP), Sixth: Dave Nourish (Enfield JAP).
>
> 500cc final – First: Martin Tatum (JAP), Second: Len Bayliss (Ellbee Special), Third: Wally Monckton (JAP), Fourth: Maurice Wilkinson (Triumph JAP), Fifth: Denys Goodacre (Triumph JAP), Sixth: Syd Mintey (Burdett Special), Seventh: Pete Elvin (AJS), Eighth: Tony Swift (Triumph JAP).
>
> Sidecar final – First: Bill Evans (Norton), Second: Harold Hill (Norton JAP), Third: John Warren (Norton JAP), Fourth: Mike Lane (JAP), Fifth: Hilton Woodrow (JAP).

Other solo competitors who did not feature in the results but helped make a truly all-star line-up included Alf Hagon, John Gould, Lew Coffin, Ralph Ellison, A.C. 'Monty' Banks (South-East), Monty Banks (South Midlands), Ray Harris, Harold 'Bill' Bridgett, Gerald Pugh and Sid Jarvis, while the sidecar event also featured Freddie French and Bert Brett.

Turning to some of the other events of 1955, it was certainly a year to remember for George Gould, who won the Southern Centre's Individual title, plus the Evesham Club's Worcestershire Championship. The Southern Centre showpiece meeting was run by the Bournemouth Club at Roke Down, with a reported crowd of 3,500 in attendance. Keeping it in the family, George's brother John took the 350cc crown, leading future Southern Centre Champion Lew Coffin home. Other categories saw Salisbury's Mike Lane retain the sidecar title, while Blackmore Vale won the annual Team Shield award. A summary of the results follows:

125cc final – First: P.J. Horner (BSA), Second: J. Dunford (BSA), Third:
  R. Hancock (BSA).
250cc final – First: Arthur Harris (Triumph), Second: D. Kelly (Triumph),
  Third: Ivor England (DOT).
350cc final – First: John Gould (Excelsior JAP), Second: Lew Coffin (JAP),
  Third: Eddie Blackwell (Royal Enfield JAP).
Up to 1,000cc final – First: George Gould (Royal Enfield JAP), Second: Eddie
  Blackwell (Royal Enfield JAP), Third: P. Bennett (JAP).
Sidecar final – First: Mike Lane (Norton JAP), Second: P. Sharples (Triumph),
  Third: R. Rhodes (Ariel).

Looking at the podium finishers, both Arthur Harris and Ivor England went on to win many scrambles awards. The meeting also included the interestingly titled Non-Championship Experts Up to 1,000cc final, and this was clearly some race, as George Gould and Lew Coffin finished in a dead-heat for first place, with Eddie Blackwell occupying third position.

The Eltham Club ran the South-Eastern Centre Championships at Frinsted in Kent, with Alf Hagon taking the major title from Pete Mitchell, while Hilton Woodrow beat off the challenge of Freddie French to win the sidecars. The results were:

125cc final – First: Ted Stokes (BSA), Second: A. Smith (BSA), Third: Geoff
  Daniels (Villiers Bantam).
250cc final – First: Pete Mitchell (JAP), Second: Roy Golding (Rudge), Third:
  Arne Hendriksen (Special).
350cc final – First: Arne Hendriksen (Special), Second: Alf Hagon (Deuble
  Special), Third: Pete Mitchell (JAP).
500cc final – First: Pete Elvin (JAP), Second: Pat Sims (JAP), Third: J. Duckett
  (BSA).
Individual final – First: Alf Hagon (Deuble Special), Second: Pete Mitchell (JAP),
  Third: Pete Elvin (JAP).
Sidecar final – First: Hilton Woodrow (JAP), Second: Freddie French (Norton),
  Third: Les Tyrell (Norton).

Staying in the South-East, the Sittingbourne Club staged four of their prestigious Silver Helmet events at Wrinsted Court, with Martin Tatum collecting two victories, while Arne Hendriksen and Sid Jarvis gained a win apiece. There was plenty going on in the area throughout the year, with meetings also held at Pleystowe Farm, Capel, near Tonbridge, Kent (Surrey Hills Club); Middle Barn Farm, Pulborough, Sussex (Horsham Club); Randalls Park (Leatherhead Club) and at Russell Place Farm, Wood Street, near Guildford (Witley Club).

In 2002 Graham Hurry and the Astra Club brought racing back to a famous venue at Rhodes Minnis, near Lyminge, Kent, and back in 1955 the Folkestone Club had started organizing events in the area at the Gate Inn. A series of race meetings were also held at Dry Hill Farm, Dormansland, Surrey, run by the East Grinstead and Owls Racing

Jimmy Rogers (29) leading the way at Stokenchurch.

Association. These took place on 29 May, 12 June, 24 July and 18 September, with the latter attracting an audience of 2,000, who witnessed Arne Hendriksen win three solo finals, and Hilton Woodrow twice triumph in sidecar races.

In Gloucestershire the September-staged Long Newnton Grand Prix resulted in victory for Geoff Pymar, ahead of Lew Coffin, Ray Harris and Gerald Pugh. The first-placed man initially began racing on grass some twenty-five years earlier, and was to enjoy an elongated speedway career after breaking into the Wimbledon side in 1933. Indeed, Pymar didn't hang up his leathers until 1962, following a stint with Bradford. In between, he raced for a couple of other London clubs, namely New Cross and Harringay, prior to spending varying lengths of time with Bristol, Norwich, Yarmouth, Middlesbrough and Wolverhampton. Speedway and grass-track have always run side by side, and aside from Pymar, each of the top four at Long Newton tried their luck at both disciplines. Coffin dabbled at Bristol, Exeter and Weymouth, while Ray Harris predominantly represented Stoke and Swindon, and Pugh raced for Cardiff, Southampton and Weymouth.

The Minety Vale Club's track at Long Newnton measured in at 530 yards in 1955, and top riders to demonstrate their skills at the venue during the season included Doug

Drewett, Bill Hopkins, Wally Monckton, the Gould brothers, Mike Keen, Ray Beaumont, George Bewley, Don Summers, Bob Jones and Len Bayliss. Several of these also appeared in speedway circles, while Don Summers was later to join Ian Paskin and Gerry Goodwin in the works Elstar team.

Top sidecar racing wasn't left off the agenda at Long Newnton either, with ace drivers Bill Evans, Harold Hill, Mike Lane, Chris Vincent, John Lidgate, John Browne, Vic Artus, Tommy Westwood and Cliff Hazell to mention but a few who raced at the venue during the year. Interestingly, Hazell and passenger Taffy Thomas used a Douglas engine on their outfit, in contrast to the more popular Nortons and JAPs of the era.

In the Midlands, the Evesham Club ran at both Pinvin, near Pershore, and at Bidford-on-Avon, over the border in Warwickshire. Staying in Warwickshire, the Stratford-upon-Avon Club held meetings at Church Farm, situated behind the railway station, while Moseley & District Motorcycle Club held their events at Hall Farm, on the Knowle-to-Kenilworth road. Wolverhampton's Wrottesley Park housed several meetings, including a charity event in aid of the PDSA (People's Dispensary of Sick Animals), when Gerry Goodwin and Len Bayliss were victorious in the solos, with Bill Evans and Harold Hill doing likewise in the sidecars. Elsewhere, on the same day, Arne Hendriksen was winning the Folkestone Championship at Rhodes Minnis, and Alf Hagon emerged triumphant from the Allcomers final at the Castle Colchester Club's meeting at Westhouse Farm, Lexden in Essex.

One of the final grass-track events to be held at Mallory Park attracted 4,000 spectators, who watched National Champion Bill Evans complete a sidecar double. Meanwhile, the Wycombe Club ran meetings at Stokenchurch on what could be described as a mountain-style circuit. These proved to be real crowd-pullers, with 3,000 watching the July meeting at which Martin Tatum and Jimmy Rogers were the solo star turns.

In the East Midlands, events were held at Allsops Lane, Loughborough; Lockwell Hill, Mansfield and at Lea Marshes, Gainsborough. The top riders at these circuits included Denys Goodacre, Syd Mintey, Dave Nourish and Len Bayliss.

Down in the Southern Centre, various meetings took place at Willoughby Hedge (Blackmore Vale Club); Totton, near Southampton; the Mount, Ringwood; Whiteway Hill (Ashton Combine), Figsbury and London Road (Salisbury Club) and of course at Roke Down (Bournemouth Club).

The South-West saw plenty of action too, with racing at Shapwick (Bridgwater Club); Bigby (Dartmouth Club); South Petherton (Yeo Vale Club); and Countess Wear, Exeter (Broadhembury Club). In Cornwall, the Pendennis Motorcycle & Light Car Club ran at Woodcock Corner, near Truro. Judging by the rider entry in the programme from this venue, led by Adrian Kessell, the majority were scramblers, which suggests the circuit was of a mountainous style.

Further up in north Cornwall, the Bude & District Motorcycle Club organized an event at Thorne Farm, Stratton, where Wally Monckton, Lew Coffin, Trevor Kessell and Adrian Kessell all collected victories. The Open final must have been a bit special though, as Coffin and Adrian Kessell dead-heated for first place. Also appearing in this meeting and starting to make a name for himself was a young man from Redruth who went by the name of Chris Blewett. He of course went on to take up speedway with

Arthur Stuffins (2) holds off a challenge from Ivor Brown at a Boston meeting, 1955.

St Austell, and later became a legend with Exeter, where his fence-scraping style is still remembered fondly to this day.

The Much Marcle Show grass-track events, originally organized by the Wye Valley Auto Club in south Herefordshire, were reputed to have started in the 1930s, although this has yet to be confirmed. Racing was certainly held in 1955, however, with the front of the programme proudly proclaiming it to be the seventy-second year of the show. Leading riders who appeared at this meeting included Reg Lambourne, Ralph Ellison, Adrian Kessell, Richie Reynolds, Roy Zeal, Lew Coffin, Tim Wall, Bill Bridgett and Austin Cresswell. That was only the tip of the iceberg as far the list of stars was concerned, as this event always attracted the top aces from all over the UK.

Other race action could be seen during 1955 on a mountain-type circuit at Coldra Farm, Chepstow, organized by the Newport & Gwent Club, while the Wigan Auto Club ran the North-West Championship at Hullet Hole Farm, Shevington. There were also venues at Cowthorpe (Wetherby), Tuxford (Retford), Whitewall Farm (Presteigne), Benton Farm, Stanford-le-Hope (Tiger Grays), Pickmere (Northwich), Quibell Park (Scunthorpe), Stapleford Tawney, Abridge (Ilford Amateur), Ottershawe, near Chertsey (Twickenham) and at Hatherton Hall Farm (Nantwich). Finally, racing was also staged in Ireland at both Belfast and Dublin.

1955 Roll of Honour

National Championships
350cc – Denys Goodacre
500cc – Martin Tatum
Sidecar – Bill Evans/Ron Jones
Inter-Centre Team (Solo) – Midlands
Inter-Centre Team (Sidecar) – East Midlands

Southern Centre Championships
125cc – P.J. Horner
250cc – Arthur Harris
350cc – John Gould
Individual – George Gould
Sidecar – Mike Lane/Bill Woodward
Team – Blackmore Vale

South Midlands Centre Championships
125cc – F. Boyce
200cc – Ernie Watson
250cc and 1,000cc – Martin Tatum
350cc – Arne Hendriksen
Sidecar – Eric Smeed
Team – Grasshopper (Chingford
Motor-Cycle Club)

South-Eastern Centre Championships
125cc – Ted Stokes
250cc – Pete Mitchell
350cc – Arne Hendriksen
500cc – Pete Elvin
1,000cc – Alf Hagon
Sidecar – Hilton Woodrow/C. Attwood

North-Western Centre Championship
Bert Lacey

East Midlands Centre Team Championship
Mansfield & District Motorcycle Club

James Mintey Memorial Trophy (Experts Barred)
Ray Bennett

Worcestershire Championship
George Gould

Long Newnton Championship
Lew Coffin

Fordham Invitation Trophy
Austin Cresswell

Eric Fernihough Trophy
Lew Coffin

Carnival Kings Sidecar Cup
Mike Lane

Cambridgeshire Championship
Austin Cresswell

North Lancashire Championship
Harry Terretta

Whipchicken Championship
Herbert Mills

Blackmore Vale Speed Trophy
Lew Coffin

Newquay Championship
Lew Coffin

Kings of Oxford Trophy
Lew Coffin

W.P. Maiden's Challenge Cup
Bill Bridgett

Folkestone Championship
Arne Hendriksen

Richmond Trophy
Syd Mintey

Yeoman's Trophy
Ivor Brown

7
GRASS-TRACK RACING
1956

The year's National Championships went to the ACU Southern Centre, being organized by the Blackmore Vale Motorcycle Club at Willoughby Hedge, near Mere. This was to be the first of many major events held by the club over the next twenty years. Several former riders were involved with the running of the meeting, including Gerald Selby (deputy clerk of the course), Wilf Sleightholme (scrutineer) and Vic Anstice (time-keeper). Meanwhile, secretary and clerk of the course was Jim Rendell, who hailed from Sutton Veny, near Warminster, and first got involved with the Blackmore Vale Club way back in 1927. Indeed, it must have been a very proud Mr Rendell on 2 September when all the track aces headed for Mere.

The club had experienced problems with the Lord's Day Observance Society, which objected to Sunday sport. To get around this situation, the Championship spectators were allowed in free of charge, with any income generated from parking fees and programme sales. Aside from that, a collection was also made by the riders, and on the front of the meeting programme it stated that all the proceeds would go to the ACU Benevolent Fund.

So to the racing, which took place on a big 1,000-yard track amid fine weather, after rain had given the circuit a good soaking in the week leading up to the event. The first action saw John Gould, appearing on home turf, take victory in a 350cc team race, with subsequent wins following for Austin Cresswell, Alf Goodey and Jim 'Jackie' Sewell. Later, in the 500cc team event, John Gould and Cresswell repeated their earlier successes, with the former keeping Alf Hagon back in the runner-up position for a second time. Hagon did, however, make up for it, taking victory in his 350cc and 500cc Championship heats, prior to emerging victorious from the final of the latter.

The 350cc final saw a close battle between two former Champions, with Austin Cresswell coming out on top after Syd Mintey had encountered mechanical difficulties. Despite his problems, Mintey still managed to hold on for second place, with local boy Lew Coffin in third spot from Dave Nourish. Completing a glorious hat-trick, the sidecar title was again claimed by Bill Evans ahead of Mike Lane, with Chris Vincent occupying third place. Briefly, referring back to the Inter-Centre Team Championships, the solo category was won by the Southern Centre, while the Midlands wrapped up the sidecar version. A summary of the results follows:

350cc final – First: Austin Cresswell (Enfield JAP), Second: Syd Mintey (Burdett Special), Third: Lew Coffin (LCS JAP), Fourth: Dave Nourish (WHB JAP).

500cc final – First: Alf Hagon (Kirby JAP), Second: Austin Cresswell (Enfield JAP), Third: John Gould (Excelsior JAP), Fourth: George Gould (Excelsior JAP).

Sidecar final – First: Bill Evans (Norton), Second: Mike Lane (JAP), Third: Chris Vincent (BSA), Fourth: Reg Cheney (Norton JAP).

Also among the tremendous array of talent on show which helped to make the solos such a rip-roaring success were grass-track greats Bill Bridgett, Eddie Blackwell, Don Summers, Wally Monckton, Dave Lane (Mike's brother), Denys Goodacre, Arthur Stuffins, Arthur Hood, A.C. 'Monty' Banks, Fred Parkins, Doug Drewett, Arne Hendriksen, Martin Tatum and Glyn Chandler. Meanwhile, the impressive field for the sidecars included John Browne, Harold Hill, Roy Cunliffe, Ken Norcutt, Freddie French, Derek Yorke and John Warren.

The big news from the year was the return of grass-track racing to Brands Hatch, with a circuit laid inside the tarmac track, in front of the grandstand. The venue was selected for the South-Eastern Centre Championships, organized by the ACU with assistance from the Eltham & District Motorcycle Club. As well as all the top regulars from the area, the meeting attracted the Gould brothers (from the Southern Centre), Austin Cresswell (Midlands) and Alf Hagon (Eastern). Also taking part was the Taitapu Special-mounted Murray Briggs, who was of course, the younger brother of speedway legend Barry. Meanwhile, another competitor was Dave Palmer, who appeared on board both Greeves and BSA scrambles machines. Having started his racing career as a scrambler, Palmer later graduated to become one of the top grass-track aces in the country.

The main event was the eight-lap solo Individual Championship, and it was Midlander Austin Cresswell on his Royal Enfield steed who took the honours from Pat Sims and Martin Tatum. Full results from the meeting were:

125cc final – First: Ray Whitling (RWS), Second: Ted Stokes (BSA), Third: F. Head (Special).

250cc final – First: Martin Tatum (Velocette), Second: Len Cooper (Cooper JAP), Third: Eric Burridge (Royal Enfield).

350cc final – First: A.C. 'Monty' Banks (B&S Special), Second: Arthur Hood (JAP), Third: George Gould (Excelsior JAP).

650cc final – First: Martin Tatum (Tatum-Ruddle Special), Second: Arne Hendriksen (Special), Third: Austin Cresswell (Royal Enfield).

Solo final – First: Austin Cresswell (Royal Enfield), Second: Pat Sims (JAP), Third: Martin Tatum (Tatum-Ruddle Special).

Sidecar final – First: P.J. Lester (Norton), Second: John Steer (JAP), Third: J.D. Sandwell (JAP).

Staying in the South-East, the Eltham and Sittingbourne Clubs had a busy season, holding seven events between them at Wrinsted Court and the Valley, Frinsted. The

SOUTH-EAST CENTRE GRASS TRACK CHAMPIONSHIP

BRANDS HATCH

ORGANIZED BY THE A.-C.U. ASSISTED BY ELTHAM & DISTRICT M.C.C.

SUNDAY, AUGUST 12, 1956

OFFICIAL PROGRAMME 2/-

Silver Helmet was contested at four of the meetings, with Sid Jarvis collecting two wins, while Lew Coffin and Arne Hendriksen were each victorious on one occasion. At the Wrinsted Court meeting in September, Coffin didn't just lift the highly sought-after Silver Helmet; he also won both the 350cc final and the Redshaw Trophy, finishing ahead of Murray Briggs and Arthur Hood in the latter. Prior to that in August, afore-mentioned scrambler Dave Palmer did well to finish as runner-up to Arne Hendriksen in the Silver Helmet.

Up in Cambridgeshire, the Ely & District Motorcycle Club ran several events, such as the Fordham Challenge Trophy on Whit Monday 21 May, when Austin Cresswell was victorious from Arthur Stuffins and Doug Drewett. Later that same week, on 26 May to be precise, they also ran a grass-track meeting at the Cambridgeshire & Ely Show, when Cresswell and Dave Nourish won two solo finals each, while Harold Hill and Derek Yorke enjoyed a win apiece in the sidecars.

The Southern Centre Championships were staged at Figsbury on 16 September, when the main individual title again saw George Gould steam to victory as he had done the year before. In the sidecars the combined talents of Mike Lane and Bill 'Sparrow' Woodward saw them to success for a fourth year in a row! Meanwhile, completing an amazing series of repeats in the prestigious event, the Team Shield was scooped by Blackmore Vale for a third successive time.

In the Western Centre, the Wye Valley Auto Club was hosting showground events. These tracks were always smaller, some being only 300 yards in length, with many of the meetings forming the 'grand finale' to a fête, flower or sports show. One of the most renowned of these was the Much Marcle & Yatton Flower Show, which was usually held on the Saturday evening of the August Bank Holiday weekend. 1956 was no exception, and brought together another top-class field of solo aces, including locals George Bewley, Gerald Pugh, Reg Lambourne, Artie Harwood and Richie Reynolds, while augmenting the line-up were three stars from further afield, namely Leo McAuliffe, Adrian Kessell and Lew Coffin.

Racing began with a win for Reg Lambourne from Lew Coffin in the 350cc heats, followed by a victory for Bill Bridgett over George Bewley. The final subsequently resulted in success for Lambourne ahead of Bridgett, with Bewley occupying third position. Next up was the Hereford Challenge Trophy for 500cc machines, with Kessell, Bridgett, Coffin and Fred Parkins all collecting heat wins. It looked like the final would again be between Lambourne and Bridgett after both claimed victories in the semis. However it didn't turn out that way, as Parkins dashed away to win from Lambourne, with Coffin in third spot.

Fred Parkins followed that up by again defeating Reg Lambourne in the Open Championship, with Bill Bridgett finishing third. That set things up nicely for the main event, which was for the Much Marcle Silver Challenge Cup. In the heats, rather predictably, there were wins for Parkins, Lambourne, Coffin and Bewley. But surprisingly, Parkins was eliminated at the semi-final stage, and it was Lambourne who went on to cover himself in glory. Results from the latter stages follow:

1956 NATIONAL
GRASS TRACK CHAMPIONSHIPS
WILLOUGHBY HEDGE, MERE, WILTS
SUNDAY, SEPTEMBER 2, 1956

By kind permission J. S. BAIN. Esq.
ALL PROCEEDS to the A.C.U. BENEVOLENT
FUND. Organised by Blackmore Vale M.C.C.
on behalf of the AUTO CYCLE UNION

OFFICIAL PROGRAMME
1/-

MOTORCYCLING

Thursdays Ninepence

Read Wherever Motorcycles are Ridden

In conjunction with
THE FORDHAM SPORTS ASSOCIATION
Present the

FORDHAM CHALLENGE TROPHY
GRASS TRACK MEETING
on
Whit-Monday, May 21st, 1956
at 2.30 p.m.

AN OPEN TO SOUTH MIDLAND CENTRE EVENT
Under G.C.R's. and Regulations of A.C.U.   Permit No. N.1538

Official Programme

OFFICIALS
A.C.U. Centre Steward: A. H. COOPER
Club Stewards: F. ALLEN and F. GOLDING   *Starter:* D. KERRIDGE
Chief Marshal: V. BARKER   *Timekeeper:* A. LEE
Competitors' Stewards: C. SARGENT and D. BELL   *Machine Examiner:* R. HOLLAND
Clerks of the Course: P. ROBERTS and A. J. PARRY
Secretary of the Meeting: A. J. PARRY, 1, New Barns Road, Ely.
Announcer and Commentator: H. W. FRIZELL

*Our best thanks are due to the Littleport St. John Ambulance Brigade for their attendance
here today*

Public Address by WRIGHT'S OF CAMBRIDGE

WARNING
Motor Racing is dangerous. You are present at this Meeting entirely at your own risk
and this programme is issued subject to the condition that all persons having any connection with the promotion and/or organisation and/or conduct of the meeting, including
the owners of the land and drivers and owners of the vehicles and passengers in the
vehicles are absolved from all liability in respect of personal injury (whether fatal or
otherwise) to you or damage to your property however caused.

W. Jefferson & Son Ltd., Printers, Ely

First Semi-final – First: Lew Coffin, Second: Austin Cresswell, Third: J. James.
Second Semi-final – First: Reg Lambourne, Second: George Bewley, Third: Bill
    Bridgett.
Final – First: Reg Lambourne, Second: Lew Coffin, Third: George Bewley.

A brief cross-section of other venues where the sport was seen during the year included
Overstone Park (Rushden), Middle Barn Farm (Horsham), Pleystowe Farm, Capel
(Surrey Hills), the Mount (Ringwood), Hams Field (Chard) and Westfields Farm
(Totton).

One of the final meetings of the year was the Ray Beaumont Testimonial, staged in
memory of the top rider who died after a track crash at Newquay in August. The
meeting took place at Wellington, near Hereford on 14 October, and saw Ray Harris
collect two solo victories, while Lew Coffin picked up a solitary success. Meanwhile, in
the sidecars, there was a brace of wins for Chris Vincent, and one for Bill Evans.

1956 Roll of Honour

National Championships
350cc – Austin Cresswell
500cc – Alf Hagon
Sidecar – Bill Evans/Ron Jones
Inter-Centre Team (Solo) – Southern
Inter-Centre Team (Sidecar) – Midlands

Southern Centre Championships
Individual – George Gould
Sidecar – Mike Lane/Bill Woodward
Team – Blackmore Vale

South Midlands Centre Championships
125cc – Mike Gutsell
200cc – Monty Banks
250cc and 500cc – Pete Mitchell
350cc – Ernie Watson
Sidecar – Freddie French/George Wasley

South-Eastern Centre Championships
125cc – Ray Whitling
250cc and 650cc – Martin Tatum
350cc – A.C. 'Monty' Banks
Solo – Austin Cresswell
Sidecar – P. Lester

Eastern Centre Championships
250cc – Frank Harker
350cc – Jack Hubbard
1,000cc – E. Green
Sidecar – Derek Yorke/George Mason

Cheshire Centre Championship
Vic Harris

East Midlands Centre Team Championship
Nottingham Tornado

Fordham All-Comers Trophy
Austin Cresswell

Cambridgeshire Championship
Austin Cresswell

W.P. Maiden's Challenge Cup
Austin Cresswell & Harold Sansby
(joint-first)

Folkestone Championship
Arne Hendriksen

Richmond Trophy
Fred Mortimer

Redshaw Trophy
Lew Coffin

Loughborough Challenge Cup
Denys Goodacre

Bridgwater Club Championship
Lew Coffin

Ludlow Trophy
Andy Lee

Ray Beaumont Memorial
Solo – Ray Harris
Sidecar – Chris Vincent/Ian Paskin

8
GRASS-TRACK RACING
1957

The year's National Championships moved over to the South Midlands, organized on behalf of the ACU by the Wycombe & District Motorcycle Club, and held at the renowned Chiltern Hills circuit in Stokenchurch, Buckinghamshire. An estimated audience of 6,000 watched Martin Tatum complete a marvellous double, taking the 350cc and 500cc solo titles, despite the close attentions of Hampshire's John Gould, who pushed him all the way in both categories. In the sidecar competition, the amazing Bill Evans and Ron Jones combination took their fourth National Championship on the trot, finishing ahead of Chris Vincent and Ian Paskin and Mike Lane and Bill Woodward. In scoring 42 points, the Inter-Centre Team Championship was dominated by the Midlands, who included two of the aforementioned rostrum-placed drivers in Evans and Vincent, with their side completed by Alf Ellis. Meanwhile, filling second position in the event on 23 points were the Southern Centre, who were represented by Mike Lane, Ken Norcutt and John Browne. In a real spread of the trophies, the solo team award went to the South-East, who recorded 39 points and boasted Martin Tatum, Murray Briggs, Eric Burridge and Pat Sims in their line-up. Having accumulated 33 points, the Southern Centre again had to be satisfied with the runner-up spot, their side consisting of Lew Coffin, Ron Goulding and the Gould brothers. The official results of the day follow:

> 350cc final – First: Martin Tatum (JAP), Second: John Gould (Excelsior JAP), Third: Alf Goodey (Enfield JAP), Fourth: Alf Hagon (Kirby JAP), Fifth: Doug Drewett (JAP), Sixth: Eddie Bayley (JAP).
> 500cc final – First: Martin Tatum (JAP), Second: John Gould (Excelsior JAP), Third: Austin Cresswell (Enfield JAP), Fourth: Eric Burridge (JAP), Fifth: George Gould (Excelsior JAP), Sixth: Maurice Wilkinson (JAP).
> Sidecar final – First: Bill Evans/Ron Jones (Norton), Second: Chris Vincent/Ian Paskin (BSA), Third: Mike Lane/Bill Woodward, Fourth: Alf Ellis/ J. Tanner (Norton).

In the South Midlands Championships, Eddie Bayley was consistency personified in taking two second places behind Arthur Sweby (250cc) and Doug Drewett (1,000cc). It could have been a hat-trick of runner-up placings too for the JAP-mounted racer but for a superb overtake of Roger Elmore which took him to victory in the 350cc class. The event, organized by the Watford & Bushey Club, was staged at Pedley Hill in Hertfordshire, and also saw successes for R. Doggett and George Markey in the 125cc and 200cc categories respectively. The Team Championship was claimed by the Southall Club, who totalled 52 points, with Grasshopper (Chingford) taking second place on 29 points, ahead of Watford and Bushey (16). The full results were:

> 125cc final – First: R. Doggett (BSA), Second: Mike Gutsell (BSA),
>   Third: R. Ford (James).
> 200cc final – First: George Markey (James), Second: Reg Nash (Greeves),
>   Third: Ken Greer (Triumph).
> 250cc final – First: Arthur Sweby (Special), Second: Eddie Bayley (JAP),
>   Third: D. Ball (JAP).
> 350cc final – First: Eddie Bayley (JAP), Second: Roger Elmore (Special),
>   Third: Jimmy Rogers (JAP).
> 1,000cc final – First: Doug Drewett (JAP), Second: Eddie Bayley (JAP),
>   Third: Doug Rolph (JAP).
> Sidecar final – First: Freddie French (Norton), Second: G. Moorcock (Special),
>   Third: Ken Norcutt (Ariel).

The South-Eastern Centre Championships took place at Pleystowe Farm in Capel, administered by the Surrey Hills Club, with Martin Tatum completing another glorious double in taking the 350cc and 650cc finals. Meanwhile there were also wins for Roy Golding in the 200cc class, Pat Sims in the 250cc category and Johnny Steer in the sidecars.

Remaining in the South-East, the Sittingbourne Club ran at Wrinsted Court, while the Eltham Club hosted events at the Valley in Frinsted. Eric Burridge (twice), Cyril Williams and Martin Tatum all collected Silver Helmet victories, while Jack Colver (Matchless) defeated Monty Banks and Sid Jarvis to win the Redshaw Trophy in September. Lew Coffin made the trip up from the South-West for at least three meetings and at the 12 July event he established a new track record of 61.50mph when winning the 500cc final ahead of Eric Burridge and speedway superstar Barry Briggs.

Riders to do well at the South-East during the year included Pat Sims, Geoff Daniels, John Argrave, Jack Colver, Sid Jarvis, Cyril Williams, Don Godden, Ted Stokes and Monty Banks. One interesting result was Barry Briggs' July victory in the Barham Championship, ahead of local ace Sid Jarvis.

Although fewer meetings were held in the Southern Centre throughout the year, racing was seen at Dean Hill (Romsey & District Motorcycle and Light Car Club); Westfield Farm, Totton; The Mount, Ringwood and at Willoughby Hedge. The Goulds, Lew Coffin and Fred Parkins were the men to beat in the solos, while the leading sidecar outfit was the Mike Lane and Sparrow Woodward combination.

There was plenty going on in the Eastern Centre, with attendances of up to 4,000 reported. Among the clubs staging meetings were Ilford Amateur Motorcycle Club (Abridge), the Tigers Club from Grays (Stanford-le-Hope), ESSA (Chelmsford) and Bedford Eagles (Houghton Conquest). Interestingly, the Eastern Sporting Sidecar Association ran an event at Montpelliers Farm, Writtle on 29 September, when the sidecar

Early days for Ken Norcutt and Brian Peeling (61) at a Ringwood event, 1957.

entry included the combination of Dave Bickers and Clive Noy, mounted on board a 500cc BSA outfit. Bickers, of course, went on to become European 250cc Scrambles Champion, while Noy became an Eastern Centre solo ace, as well as appearing in speedway circles for both Ipswich and Peterborough. Meanwhile a solo rider destined for great things arrived on the scene in the area during 1957, namely Ian Towns, mounted on a 197cc DOT.

Another renowned racetrack was the Braintree & District Motorcycle Club's circuit at Lyons Hall, Bocking. A meeting at the venue on 27 July brought no less than five final victories for Arthur Stuffins, the Peterborough rider, who was to go down as a legend in the East Midlands area, becoming known as the 'King of the Showgrounds'.

Having mentioned the East Midlands, the area was a hotbed for the sport, with clubs and venues including Ely & District Motorcycle Club (who ran at both the County Showground in Dullingham and at Sutton Sports Field), Spalding Club (Clay Lake Field), Peterborough Club (at both Whittlesey and also at Wansford), Grantham Pegasus Motorcycle & Light Car Club (Woodnook), Wisbech Club (Walsoken), Hunts Falcons (St Ives) and Retford Club (Tuxford). Aside from those sites, racing was also hosted at Lea Marshes in Gainsborough, and at Allsops Lane, Loughborough.

The leading riders to do battle in this neck of the woods included Arthur Stuffins, Denys Goodacre, Harold Sansby, Dave Nourish, Jackie Sewell, Ken Greer (the father of future grass and speedway star Richard) and Ivor Brown, who later went on to become a speedway hero at both Yarmouth and Cradley Heath in the Provincial League. Former National 350cc Champion Syd Mintey also rode in the area, and was still winning races too.

Down in the far South-West, race meetings were held at the Newquay Club's Quintrell Downs raceway, as well as at the small 250-yard Exeter Vikings track. At these events Cornishmen Adrian Kessell and Chris Julian did battle against such riders as Fred Parkins and Lew Coffin.

Only the Minety Vale Club was running in the Wessex Centre, at their Long Newnton Aerodrome venue. 5,000 fans flocked to the circuit to witness an all-star line-up compete for the Long Newnton Championships, which saw Martin Tatum scoop first place in four of the finals, although he could only finish third in the main solo event behind brothers John and George Gould. Hereford's Ray Harris did well too, finishing in the top five in all his finals, with the Non-Winners final being won by Pershore's George Bewley. The masterful Bill Evans and partner Ron Jones wrapped up the Sidecar Championship, although in the first such final of the day they were beaten into third position by the combinations of Chris Vincent and Ian Paskin and Mike Lane and Bill Woodward. The main Championships resulted thus:

> Solo final – First: John Gould, Second: George Gould, Third: Martin Tatum,
>   Fourth: Ray Harris.
> Sidecar final – First: Bill Evans, Second: Chris Vincent, Third: C. Evans.

Over the border, George Bewley pulled off the best win of his career thus far when he took the prestigious Worcestershire Championship at Ham Dean Farm, Pinvin. On a wet and slick 500-yard oval track, Bill Bridgett (350cc) and Ray Harris (500cc) were the earlier winners, but in the main Championship, run over ten laps, Bewley defeated Bridgett by half-a-wheel, while Harris was forced out by mechanical gremlins, thereby allowing local ace Austin Cresswell to mop up third place. The aforementioned Cresswell quickly made up for his third place in the big Worcestershire event, however, by winning the Warwickshire Championship at Stratford-upon-Avon.

The Wye Valley Auto Club, Ledbury Cobras, and the Ross & District Clubs were all proactive with the Herefordshire showgrounds, which provided fantastic shoulder-to-shoulder, wheel-to-wheel action on the short, fast ovals. Some of the results were:

> Much Marcle Challenge Cup (Wye Valley Auto Club, at the Much Marcle Show) –
>   First: Fred Parkins, Second: Ray Harris, Third: Lew Coffin.
> Hereford Challenge Cup (Wye Valley Auto Club, at the Much Marcle Show) –
>   First: Fred Parkins, Second: Reg Lambourne, Third: Lew Coffin.
> Bishop Bevan Challenge Cup (Wye Valley Auto Club, at Woolhope Sports
>   Show) – First: Artie Harwood, Second: Bill Bridgett, Third: Austin Cresswell.
> Withington & District Challenge Cup (Ross & District Club, at the Withington
>   Show) – First: Lew Coffin, Second: Artie Harwood, Third: Austin Cresswell.
> Unlimited final (Ross & District Club, Broad Oak, near Monmouth) – First: Ken
>   Williams, Second: Lew Coffin, Third: George Bewley.
> Hopkins Silver Challenge Cup (Ledbury Cobras, at Ledbury Floral Fête) –
>   First: Ray Harris, Second: Austin Cresswell, Third: Bill Bridgett.

Racing was still popular in Ireland, where Billy Hutton rode constantly in grass-track, trials and scrambles racing. Here, he is pictured on a Matchless scrambles machine, as ever sporting the number 25.

Before finishing with showgrounds, it is worth mentioning the Kilburn Feast in Yorkshire. In 1957, like many other years, grass-track racing was featured at this weekend festival. The Thirsk Club ran the meeting on a 440-yard circuit, with Roy Cunliffe emerging as the victor from the main sidecar event. Meanwhile, winning the Unlimited solo category was scrambler and BSA-works rider Arthur Lampkin.

In the North-West, grass action was staged at Carnforth, Lancashire, while on the other side of the Dales, racing was held at Pickering. At the latter venue's June meeting, future Middlesbrough and Halifax Speedway teamster Dave Younghusband was the star of the show, winning the 200cc final in front of a 2,000 crowd. Staying in Yorkshire, the Rotherham & District Motor Club organized meetings at Clifton Park. Remarkably, they actually ran two meetings on 6 August, one at 3 p.m., while the other began at 6.30 p.m. The afternoon meeting saw speedway rider Maurice 'Slant' Payling of Belle Vue emerge victorious from two of the finals.

1957 Roll of Honour

National Championships
350cc and 500cc – Martin Tatum
Sidecar – Bill Evans/Ron Jones
Inter-Centre Team (Solo) – South-East
Inter-Centre Team (Sidecar) – Midlands

Southern Centre Championships
250cc – Arthur Harris
350cc – John Gould
Individual – John Gould
Sidecar – Mike Lane/Bill Woodward
Team – Blackmore Vale

South Midlands Centre Championships
125cc – R. Doggett
200cc – George Markey
250cc – Arthur Sweby
350cc – Eddie Bayley
1,000cc – Doug Drewett
Sidecar – Freddie French/George Wasley
Team – Southall

South-Eastern Centre Championships
200cc – Roy Goulding
250cc – Pat Sims
350cc and 650cc – Martin Tatum
Sidecar – Johnny Steer/W. Davidson

Eastern Centre Championships
250cc – K. Lewis
350cc – Alf Hagon
1,000cc – Jack Hubbard
Sidecar – Tom Appleton/C. Pollington
Team – Braintree

East Midlands Centre Team Championship
Nottingham Tornado

Huntingdonshire Championships
350cc – Doug Rolph
500cc – Austin Cresswell
Sidecar – Dave Nourish/Rob Williamson

Irish Championships
200cc – B. Rodgers
350cc and 500cc – Arthur Clarke

Worcestershire Championship
George Bewley

Warwickshire Championship
Austin Cresswell

Fordham Trophy
Bill Bridgett

Redshaw Trophy
Jack Colver

Loughborough Challenge Cup
Denys Goodacre

Ludlow Trophy
Andy Lee

Ray Beaumont Memorial
Fred Parkins

Carnival Kings Sidecar Cup
Bill Evans/Ron Jones

Long Newnton Championships
Solo – John Gould
Sidecar – Bill Evans/Ron Jones

Willoughby Hedge Championships
350cc – Fred Parkins
Individual – Lew Coffin

Knowle Championships
Solo – Austin Cresswell
Sidecar – Bill Evans/Ron Jones

Withington Show Challenge Trophy
Lew Coffin

Richmond Trophy
Jackie Sewell

Hopkins Silver Challenge Cup
Ray Harris

Bishop Bevan Challenge Cup
Artie Harwood

Much Marcle Show Challenge Cup
Fred Parkins

Barham Championship
Barry Briggs

Ken Smith Trophy
Sid Jarvis

Don Davis Memorial Trophy
Roy Hartop

Dave Bach Memorial Left-Hand Sidecar Trophy
Freddie French/George Wasley

Invicta Championship
Sid Jarvis

Broadhembury Trophy
Lew Coffin

Gunnell Trophy
Jimmy Rogers

Ely Show Championships
350cc and 1,000cc – Bill Bridgett

Whittlesey Show Challenge Cup
Bill Bridgett

Clifton Park Trophy
Arthur Stuffins

Chris Vincent (250) won the 1958 National title with Don Summers at Willoughby Hedge. He is pictured here with Ian Paskin at the same venue at a later date.

9
GRASS-TRACK RACING
1958

It was back to the Southern Centre for the National Championships, with a new track being used by the Blackmore Vale Club at Willoughby Hedge. The meeting saw Murray Briggs complete a wonderful double, winning the 350cc and 500cc titles on an 880-yard kidney-shaped racing circuit. The major honours certainly didn't look like going the way of Briggs earlier in the meeting though, as he had suffered defeat at the hands of Jackie Sewell and Lew Coffin in the second heat of the 500s. However, in the 350cc event, 'Briggo' junior beat off the challenges of Martin Tatum for victory, with John Gould finishing third. The 500cc final brought Briggs a slice of luck, as Bill Bridgett and Tatum both went out, having initially led. Meanwhile, John Gould again scooped a podium position after an exciting exchange with Coffin.

The winning South-Eastern (solo) team at the 1958 National Championships. From left to right: Sid Jarvis, Eric Burridge, Murray Briggs, Martin Tatum and Cyril Williams. Also pictured with the trophy is team manager Jim Walby.

In the sidecars, Bill Evans wasn't able to retain his title after shedding a chain while he battled with fellow Midlander Chris Vincent on the first bend. Vincent, who later went on to road-race and TT fame, eventually took the chequered flag from Freddie French and Keith Blaynee. The solo version of the Inter-Centre Team Championship was won by the South-East, who were strongly represented by Martin Tatum, Murray Briggs, Sid Jarvis, Cyril Williams and Don Godden. Between them they accumulated 32 points, with the Southern Centre in second place on 29 points, and the Midlands third on a total of 27. The sidecar team trophy was wrapped up by the Midlands, who raced to 56 points, and with Chris Vincent, Keith Blaynee and Bill Evans in the side, it was easy to see why they came out on top. The South Midlands finished as runners-up on 26 points, while a tally of 21 was sufficient for the Southern Centre to occupy third spot. The major results of the Nationals follow:

> 350cc final – First: Murray Briggs (Taitapu JAP), Second: Martin Tatum (TR JAP), Third: John Gould (JAP), Fourth: Bill Bridgett (JAP).
> 500cc final – First: Murray Briggs (Taitapu JAP), Second: John Gould (JAP), Third: Lew Coffin (LCS JAP), Fourth: Dave Nourish (WHB JAP).
> Sidecar final – First: Chris Vincent/Don Summers (BSA), Second: Freddie French/George Wasley (Norton), Third: Keith Blaynee/G. Sanders (BSA), Fourth: John Warren/J. Gibbins (BSA).

The South-East area was just getting stronger and stronger, both in terms of riders and events. At the Sittingbourne Club's meetings the Silver Helmet was again raced for, with two wins for Martin Tatum and one for Don Godden. There were often many exciting tussles for the coveted trophy, none more so than the ones involving Lew Coffin and Martin Tatum. Other events in the area were staged at Rhodes Minnis, Ashford, East Grinstead, Barham, Lydden, Pulborough and Ramsgate. Top stars like Arne Hendriksen, Jack Colver, Cyril Williams, Eric Burridge, Alf Hagon, Murray Briggs and Monty Banks all tasted victory at these meetings, along with the previously mentioned duo of Tatum and Godden.

Some of the first action of the season was staged by the Invicta Club at Tubbs Corner, Sandwich, near Ramsgate, which produced a 500cc victory for South-West raider Lew Coffin. The Gould brothers also paid a couple of visits to the South-East during the year, appearing at Pleystowe Farm, Capel on 20 April and Middle Barn Farm, Horsham on 26 May. At the former, John Gould was victorious in the 350cc final ahead of Midland visitor Austin Cresswell, and the third-placed Martin Tatum. Later in the meeting, a change to the finishing order saw Tatum win the 650cc category from Gould and Arne Hendriksen. Then, just to spread the victories around, Cresswell defeated Gould and Tatum in the 9-Fastest final. Just for the record, Jack Colver (200cc) and Sid Jarvis (250cc) were the other lightweight solo final winners at the meeting, which was well organized by the Surrey Hills Club. Turning to the sidecars, South Midlander Freddie French took two victories, with the other going to John Steer. Interestingly a name for the future secured a runner-up placing in the 500cc Invitation Handicap, namely Stan Luck, who would go on to become 350cc National Champion in 1973.

In Ireland, the Gold Star-mounted Alex Woods (98) had been the man to beat in the 350cc class after the war. He retired in the 1950s, but later made a comeback to the grass scene.

There were numerous meetings in the East Midlands and Eastern Centres, where Alf Hagon, Tony Sutton, Arthur Stuffins, Denys Goodacre, Arthur Pell, Jackie Sewell, Harold Sansby, Ken Greer, Dave Nourish and Gethin Johnson were just some of the grass legends to do battle. Arne Hendriksen, Martin Tatum, Austin Cresswell and a few other leading riders also paid visits to these areas to take some of the spoils of victory. Meanwhile, with regard to the sidecars, Bill Evans, Chris Vincent and Harold Hill proved to be regular winners in the East Midlands sector.

The South Midlands Centre had its fair share of racing too, with the Watford Club's circuit at Cassiobury Park and the Wycombe Club's track at Chiltern Hills, Stokenchurch being particularly popular with riders and spectators alike. Vintage races had started to be held by both clubs, and one such event was run at Stokenchurch on 6 July, when A. Morgan, mounted on board a 1930 Rudge machine, took victory from F. Heath and E. Thompson.

There weren't so many meetings in the South-West, but racing was staged by the Newquay, Broadhembury, Dartmouth and Bridgwater Clubs. Top riders to lift trophies in the area were Lew Coffin, Adrian Kessell and Fred Parkins, while two lads from Penhale were always there or thereabouts, namely Eric Roberts and Chris Julian.

Further up-country in Gloucestershire, racing was held by the Dowty Motor Club at Climperwell Park, near Birdlip, and by the West Gloucester & Dean Forest Auto Club at Lydney. At the Dowty Club's May meeting, the honours were split between Austin Cresswell and George Bewley, plus the scrambling twosome of Tom Barker and Roy King, with Trevor Plant taking victory in the Non-Winners final. The Climperwell Park circuit was of a mountain style, and among other riders who enjoyed its challenges were top scrambler and Swindonian Ken Messenger, plus Gloucester's Chris Healey, whose son, Tim, has been doing well on grass in the modern era, while also trying to break into speedway. Roger Elmore was another to compete at the Birdlip venue, his efforts forming only a small part of an elongated racing career that spanned an amazing six decades. Terry Sleeman and Jim Timms were also identified at the circuit, although both were better known for their scrambling exploits.

On 2 August at Lydney Bill Bridgett was in a class of his own, remarkably winning four finals, with the remaining honours going to George Bewley (250cc) and T. Smith (Handicap). Among others to finish high up in the results were Lew Coffin and John Gould, but they could only battle with each other for the position of runner-up behind the flying Bridgett.

Despite the successes of Birdlip and Lydney, it was still Long Newnton that attracted the cream of the grass-track aces to the 600-yard airfield track. A series of meetings were staged by the Minety Vale Club at the famous venue during the year, all of which attracted 4,000-5,000 spectators. On 18 May, Martin Tatum paid a visit and won most of the finals, including the Long Newnton Laurels. He did suffer one loss, however, when Ray Harris beat him in the Club Scratch final, but the likes of Lew Coffin, Fred Parkins, the Goulds and Jimmy Rogers just couldn't get near the man affectionately known as 'Spud'.

Later, on 22 June, Tatum didn't feature in the entry list, and the honours were shared around with victories for Fred Parkins (350cc final), Lew Coffin (500cc final), Ray Harris (Grand Prix final), and Jim Gale (Non-Winners final). Sidecar king Bill Evans was a regular victor at the circuit, and at the final meeting of the year on 27 September he took on and defeated another fifteen outfits to lift the Long Newnton Championship in wet conditions. It certainly was a class field, for the line-up included Harold Hill, Chris Vincent, Ray Gerring, Ken Fisher, Keith Blaynee, Alf Ellis, Mike Lane, Ken Norcutt and John Browne.

Staying with the fabulous airfield raceway, the season's grand finale attracted a top-notch field for the Long Newnton Solo Championship, with the Battle of Britain Trophy up for grabs. The wetness of the racing strip clearly caught out several of the leading names, but it was the JAP-mounted Ray Harris who mastered the conditions to take victory from Ron Taylor, Murray Briggs and Lew Coffin. To complete the picture, the other finals at the event went the way of Jackie Sewell (350cc) and George Bewley (500cc).

Moving into Wales, racing was organized by the Presteigne Auto Club at three circuits, namely Home Farm, Norton; Island Farm, Brecon and at Rhayader. Bill Bridgett, Austin Cresswell, George Bewley and Ray Harris were all winners in the Principality, while

Three racers on a fast corner at Willoughby Hedge, with John Brickell (26) leading from Tony Chant. The third ace is the brave man in the centre, ex-rider turned photographer Cecil Bailey.

competitors from the home country included Roy Zeal and Cyril Francis. Another Welsh venue that hosted racing on and off from the 1930s to 1986 was Carmarthen Park. This really was some track, situated around a rugby pitch with a banked concrete cycle track on the outside. Just imagine the scene at a 1958 race meeting, when a crowd of 5,000 spectators were able to look down on the racing below and witness victories for local riders R. Rees (250cc final), Lloyd Tucker (350cc final), T. Jones (Unlimited final) and C. Watkins (Grass Machines Only final). However, it wouldn't be long before the likes of Ron Taylor, Lew Coffin and the other top riders found out about this fantastic circuit, and of course the good prize money on offer!

The tight little Hereford showground circuits again served up thrilling wheel-to-wheel action during the year. Fred Parkins cleaned up at the Bosbury Show, defeating Lew Coffin, Bill Bridgett and Ray Harris to win all four finals. At the Grafton Show it was Harris who took three finals, while at the Ledbury Show the Hereford man collected a further brace of victories, with Bridgett winning the other final – all this in front of an estimated audience of some 4,000. Frank Evans, who had previously ridden for Bristol, Cradley Heath, Hanley and Swindon in grass-track's sister sport of speedway, had three runner-up places at Ledbury, while Cornishman Adrian Kessell notched a third.

The Withington Show saw George Bewley fend off Frank Evans and Lew Coffin to take the Challenge Cup, while the other finals of the day resulted in two wins for Bill Bridgett and one for the redoubtable Coffin. At Much Marcle it was a clean sweep for Ray Harris, with victories in the Challenge Cup, Championship and 500cc finals. Aside from Harris, the line-up included another speedway racer in Ernie Lessiter, plus future dirt-track racers Tim Bungay and Fred Powell. Sidecar racing was also included at this event, with a victory apiece for Harold Hill and Chris Vincent.

In the Southern Centre, racing was held at Willoughby Hedge, the Mount, Corhampton (Bishop's Waltham), Westfield Farm (Totton), Kingsclere Road (Basingstoke) and Dean Hill (Romsey). While Lew Coffin and John Gould won most of the solo finals at these venues, it was Jim Gale who seemed to dominate in the Experts Barred races, with the combination of Mike Lane and Bill Woodward being the sidecar kings.

Up in the Midlands tracks included Knowle (West Bromwich and Antelope Clubs), Ufton (Leamington Club), Child's Ercall (Market Drayton Club) and Pinvin (Evesham Club). Like Lew Coffin and John Gould in the South, solo aces Austin Cresswell and Bill Bridgett reigned supreme at these circuits, while the sidecar aces were Bill Evans, Chris Vincent and Harold Hill.

So to the North, where racing was held at Sutton Bank (Thirsk & District Motor Club), Clifton Park (Rotherham Club), Rocksavage (Runcorn Club), Stonebridge Fields, Skipton (Craven District Motorcycle Club) and Warton (North Lancs Club). That covers just a cross-section from east to west but gives a good indication of the activity in that particular region of the country. Maurice Wilkinson and Eric Carr were frequent victors in Yorkshire and Lancashire, while in the Cheshire area the regular winners included Jack Grindley, Keith Terretta, Paul Cross and the scrambler-mounted Arthur Lampkin. The Cheshire Centre also saw Midlanders Gerry Goodwin and Austin Cresswell win races, while East Midlands stars Jackie Sewell, Arthur Stuffins and Dave Nourish excelled on an excursion up to Rotherham in South Yorkshire.

In Ireland, racing was held at various places including Waterford, Belfast and Dublin, with Gerry Scarlett from the capital of Eire being one of the top men. Scotland hosted some grass-track racing too, with riders such as Bill Landels and Willie Templeton competing prior to later moving into the speedway scene.

Completing the overview of the season, it is worth mentioning how some of the major Championships panned out. In a meeting organized by the Watford & Bushey Club, Alf Hagon won both the 350cc and 500cc South Midlands titles at Pedley Hill, near Hemel Hempstead. Meanwhile, with George Wasley in the chair, sidecar superstar Freddie French garnered another success at the same event. Staying with sidecars, Derek Yorke took the Eastern Centre final at Abridge, while in the Southern Centre Championships Lew Coffin was the solo master, plundering a 350cc/500cc double at Ansty, near Salisbury. Other winners in the Southern Centre that day were Tim Bungay (Novice final), Eric Holcombe (250cc), and Mike Lane and Bill Woodward (sidecars). Another victor was Norman Pike in the Intermediate category, and in a link with the modern era, he of course is the father of Eric and Graham. Finally, Bill Bridgett took the Worcestershire Championship with some ease, finishing ahead of Fred Parkins and George Bewley.

1958 Roll of Honour

National Championships
350cc and 500cc – Murray Briggs
Sidecar – Chris Vincent/Don Summers
Inter-Centre Team (Solo) – South-East
Inter-Centre Team (Sidecar) – Midlands

Southern Centre Championships
250cc – Eric Holcombe
350cc and Individual – Lew Coffin
Sidecar – Mike Lane/
Bill Woodward
Team – Blackmore Vale

South Midlands Centre Championships
125cc – R. Doggett
200cc – Don Baxter
250cc – Eddie Bayley
350cc and 500cc – Alf Hagon
Sidecar – Freddie French/George Wasley
Team – Southall

South-Eastern Centre Championships
200cc – Ted Stokes
250cc – Jack Colver
350cc – Arne Hendriksen
650cc and Individual – Martin Tatum
Sidecar – Freddie French/George Wasley

Eastern Centre Championships
250cc – K. Lewis
350cc – Mick Manderville
1,000cc – K. Carrington
Sidecar – Derek Yorke/George Mason

East Midlands Centre Team Championship
Nottingham Tornado

Irish Championships
250cc – W.R. Mann
350cc and 500cc – Noel Bell

Worcestershire Championship
Bill Bridgett

Cambridgeshire Championships
Solo – Denys Goodacre
Sidecar – Keith Blaynee/G. Sanders

Fordham Trophy
350cc – Jackie Sewell
500cc – Austin Cresswell
Sidecar – Bill Evans/Ron Jones

Loughborough Challenge Cup
Denys Goodacre

Ray Beaumont Memorial
Fred Parkins

Carnival Kings Sidecar Cup
Bill Evans/Ron Jones

Long Newnton Championships
350cc – Jackie Sewell
Unlimited – Ray Harris
Sidecar – Bill Evans/Ron Jones

Knowle Championships
Solo – Austin Cresswell
Sidecar – Bill Evans/Ron Jones

Withington Show Challenge Trophy
George Bewley

Much Marcle Show Challenge Cup
Ray Harris

Dave Bach Memorial Left-Hand Sidecar Trophy
Johnny Steer/W. Davidson

Gunnell Trophy
Jimmy Rogers

Ely Show Challenge Cup
Fred Parkins

Whittlesey Show Challenge Cup
Solo – Harold Sansby
Sidecar – Keith Blaynee/G. Sanders

Clifton Park Trophy
Arthur Stuffins

Bosbury Show Challenge Cup
Fred Parkins

Grafton Show Challenge Cup
Ray Harris

Windmill Solo Cup
Arthur Stuffins

Fenland Sidecar Cup
Bill Evans/Ron Jones

Runcorn Championship
Austin Cresswell

Lydney Motorcycles Trophy
Austin Cresswell

Somerset Challenge Shield
Ray Harris

Long Newnton Laurels
Solo – Martin Tatum
Sidecar – Bill Evans/Ron Jones

Long Newnton Grand Prix
Ray Harris

Huntingdonshire County Show Championship
Joey Neath

Ledbury Challenge Trophy
Ray Harris

Spalding Golden Helmet Final
Jackie Sewell

Multi-Irish Champion Jack Agnew (204) chases after W. Walmsley (181) and R. Spence (155).

10
GRASS-TRACK RACING
1959

Hereford's Ron Taylor nearly caused a sensation as the National Championships headed for the Fens, with the meeting held by the Ely & District Motorcycle Club on behalf of the ACU at High Ridge Farm, Sutton in Cambridgeshire. The circuit was 800 yards in circumference and although the racing was good, conditions became very dusty for the competitors and the estimated 15,000 crowd in attendance.

As usual the Inter-Centre Team Championship races took place first, with the East Midlands coming out on top in the solos. The heat winners came from various centres, with Jackie Sewell (350cc and 500cc), John Gould (350cc), Bill Bridgett (350cc), Doug Drewett (350cc), Alf Hagon (500cc), Ron Taylor (500cc) and George Gould (500cc) all taking victories. However, it was the riders representing the East Midlands who proved the most consistent, their side being made up by Denys Goodacre, Dave Nourish, Ray Bennett and Jackie Sewell. Meanwhile in the sidecars, with the pairings of Freddie French/George Wasley, Doug John/Brian Jones and George Cross/Peter Horne in the team, it was the turn of the South Midlands to succeed.

In the individual events, Alf Hagon took the 350cc title ahead of John Gould, while a great scrap for third position resulted in a dead-heat between Jackie Sewell and Lew Coffin. The 500cc final was led by Ron Taylor, who at the time was only a star in his own Western Centre. Unfortunately for Taylor he went wide on a corner, letting in Hagon and Austin Cresswell, and despite fighting back to grab second spot it was the 1956 Champion who went on to complete a wonderful double. There was a new victor in the sidecars, as Freddie French and chair partner George Wasley defeated Mike Lane and Bill Woodward, with four-times previous winners Bill Evans and Ron Jones occupying third place. For French it was a well-earned success as he had started in solo trials and scrambles in the late 1940s before moving on to the sidecars. His first notable win had occurred at the South Midlands Centre Championships in 1953, and while other victories followed this was the 'big one' for French. Results from the prestigious event were:

> 350cc final – First: Alf Hagon (Kirby JAP), Second: John Gould (JAP), Equal Third: Jackie Sewell (JAP) and Lew Coffin (LCS JAP), Fifth: Reg Luckhurst (DSS JAP).

The South-Eastern (solo) team pictured at the 1959 National Championships. From left to right: Ted Jelf, Don Godden, Reg Luckhurst and Monty Banks.

500cc final – First: Alf Hagon (Kirby JAP), Second: Ron Taylor (JAP), Third: Austin Cresswell (Enfield JAP), Fourth: Tim Bungay (LCS JAP), Fifth: Arthur Stuffins (RBS JAP).

Sidecar final – First: Freddie French/George Wasley (Norton), Second: Mike Lane/Bill Woodward (JAP), Third: Bill Evans/Ron Jones (Norton), Fourth: Keith Blaynee/G. Sanders (BSA).

Team Championship (Solo) – First: East Midlands 39pts, Second: South-East 38, Third: South Midlands 35, Fourth: Southern 34.

Team Championship (Sidecar) – First: South Midlands 43pts, Second: Midlands 26, Third: South-East 18, Fourth: Southern 12.

In the South-East, the Sittingbourne Silver Helmet winners for the year were Cyril Williams (two) and Don Godden, plus a new name in Hugh Price. Really starting to fly in the region was Don Godden, and at the Astra Club's Lydden circuit he scooped three titles in the Centre Championships – 350cc, 650cc and Individual Unlimited. Mounted on a JAP, his victory in the main solo final, run over twelve laps, came at the expense of runner-up Monty Banks (B&S Special), and the third-placed Hugh Price (JAP). The sidecar event resulted in another success for the formidable duo of Freddie French and George Wasley, who retained the title they had won the previous year.

Don Godden also took the chequered flag in several other meetings including the Folkestone Championship where he defeated Monty Banks again, with Reg Luckhurst

finishing third. At the Barham event he lifted the Ken Smith Memorial Trophy after winning a twenty-lap final from Reg Luckhurst and Stan Luck. He didn't get it all his own way though, especially in the Horsham Club's meeting at Middle Barn Farm, Pulborough, when brothers John and George Gould both defeated him. As if to make sure that wasn't a one-off, John Gould repeated his success over Godden at Capel, where Alf Hagon and Reg Luckhurst also witnessed his rear wheel.

Other leading solo speedsters not previously mentioned, but who also competed in the South-East during the season, included Ted Jelf, Ted Stokes, Geoff Daniels, Arthur Wicken, Eric Burridge, Ray Whitling and Mick Philpott, while the John Steer and W. Davidson combination were particularly dominant in the sidecar class. Meanwhile, outsiders to make successful visits to the area were Lew Coffin, Bill Bridgett and Arthur Stuffins.

The aforementioned Gould brothers had so often been near to winning National titles and on several occasions only just lost out. Their battles during the 1950s against the likes of Lew Coffin, Austin Cresswell and many other top aces have gone down as legendary in the history of grass-track racing. To give an idea of how busy they were, the twosome's race programme for 1959 included meetings at Overstone Park (Rushden & District Club); Willoughby Hedge (Blackmore Vale Motorcycle Club); Pleystowe Farm (Surrey Hill Motor Club); Ansty (Salisbury Motorcycle & Light Car Club); Middle Barn Farm (Horsham & District Club); Long Newnton (Minety Vale Motor Club); Corhampton Park (Bishop's Waltham Club) and Bury Gate (Aldwick 100 Motor

Club). Aside from those meetings, the duo also appeared in the Southern Centre Championships, run by the Basingstoke Club at Kingsclere Road on 16 August, as well as the Nationals at Sutton on 6 September.

Sticking with the Gould boys, the meeting at Overstone Park took place on 30 March and represented one of the furthest journeys they made, but it was a successful trip for John, bringing three victories. Sidecar winners that day were Freddie French and Mike Lane, the latter also making the trek up to Northamptonshire. The solo events resulted as follows:

> 350cc final – First: John Gould, Second: Austin Cresswell, Third: Bill Bridgett.
> 500cc final – First: John Gould, Second: Austin Cresswell, Third: Bill Bridgett.
> Up to 1,000cc final – First: John Gould, Second: Austin Cresswell, Third: Denys Goodacre.

Having mentioned Mike Lane, who was the sidecar king in the Southern Centre, some of the other top drivers from the area in 1959 included Ken Norcutt, Viv Debben, Jack Knight, Fred Wicks, John Browne and John Callander. Turning to solos, some of the area's masters were Norman Pike, Jimmy Gale, Tim Bungay, Max Richards, John Argrave and Artie Thick. Also starting to climb the grass-track ladder were the likes of Roy Oldaker, John Trevitt and Pete Munday. It is interesting to note that leading national-standard trials rider Peter Stirland also raced in the year's Southern Centre Championships.

Talking of which, the Individual Championship was awarded over two events in one meeting at Basingstoke on 16 August, and with a win plus a second behind his brother another title was added to the shelf of John Gould in the 351-1,000cc category. That completed a fabulous double, for John also scooped the 350cc crown, defeating Austin Cresswell and Lew Coffin. The sidecar event resulted in yet another success for the pairing of Mike Lane and Sparrow Woodward, while two future speedway riders also collected victories in solo classes, namely Pete Munday (Novice final) and Tim Bungay (Experts Barred final).

Staying in the South, Staffordshire's Bill Bridgett collected three final successes at Ringwood. Meanwhile, at two Ansty meetings, Bridgett and Austin Cresswell took the honours in May, with Jimmy Gale doing the business at the July event. Meanwhile, the Reading Club ran on a mountain-style track at Farley Hill, Arborfield, and although the circuit suited the scramblers like Ray Marsh it was John Gould who triumphed in the 350cc event. At Corhampton Park there was another victory for John Gould, while Lew Coffin and Tim Bungay also sampled that winning feeling.

At the Saturday evening meeting held by the Bridport Club at Beaminster, it was again John Gould winning three of the finals, and another brace of successes came his way in the Basingstoke Carnival meet. John won yet more finals at Willoughby Hedge in April, but it was Bill Bridgett who took the major honours at the Championship event in September. Also in that month, new national star Ron Taylor was invited by Lew Coffin to try his luck in the Southern Centre, and he grasped the opportunity with both hands, completing a glorious treble at the Bournemouth Club's meeting near Wareham.

Over in the South Midlands, the Wycombe & District Motorcycle Club's popular Chiltern Hills circuit at Stokenchurch was the venue for a series of events. Racing was also staged at two places by the Watford & Bushey Club, at Farnham Royal and Pedley Hill, while the Luton Club ran at Clay Hill Farm and the Hayes Club at Charville Lane. The meeting at Clay Hill Farm was on a mountain-style track, and it was there that future Southern Centre and South Midlands Champion Dave Palmer collected a couple of victories on his scrambler. Jimmy Rogers was the regional rider to win a fair few finals at Stokenchurch, while at Farnham Royal the 250cc victor was the Velocette-mounted Peter Randall, who was another name for the future. Meanwhile, just starting out and also riding a Velocette was another Sweby, namely Arthur's son Colin.

Not only did the East Midlands win the solo team award in 1959 but they also had one of the strongest regions for on-track action, and along with the Eastern Centre there was a lot of racing for both competitors and spectators alike. The list of top-drawer riders was seemingly endless in the East Midlands and featured Jackie Sewell, Ken Greer, Denys Goodacre, Gethin Johnson, Arthur Stuffins, Norman 'Rocky' Bailey (who later moved on to sidecars), Ivor Brown, Fred Blower, Ray Bennett and Arthur Pell. Added to them were the likes of Bill Bridgett, Austin Cresswell and Arne Hendriksen, who visited the area to challenge the local hotshots.

The Spalding & Tongue End Club organized racing at Clay Lake Field, and on a circuit which produced some terrific action there were wins for Austin Cresswell, Arthur Pell and Jackie Sewell. Briefly running through a few of the other venues, Denys Goodacre won two finals at Matlock (Derwent Club), while another Spalding meeting brought a further three victories for Sewell. At Peterborough Bill Bridgett brought home the bacon, whereas at Boston it was Arthur Pell and Arthur Stuffins who were successful. Sewell was again victorious at both Retford and Diss, while Dave Nourish was a solo and sidecar winner at Wisbech.

In July, the climax of the Peterborough Agricultural Society Show saw a top-class grass-track event, featuring many of the aforementioned riders. In a meeting that was actually the first staged at the showground since the Second World War, there were sidecar wins for Bill Evans and Tony Wakefield. The remainder of the results were:

250cc final – First: Dave Nourish, Second: Bill Bridgett, Third: Arthur Stuffins.
350cc final – First: Bill Bridgett, Second: Arthur Stuffins, Third: Dave Nourish.
500cc final – First: Bill Bridgett, Second: Joey Neath, Third: Dave Nourish.
Unlimited final – First: Bill Bridgett, Second: Joey Neath, Third: Arthur Stuffins.
8-Fastest final – First: Arthur Stuffins, Second: Joey Neath, Third: Dave Nourish.

Although there were not so many meetings down in the South-West, the Broadhembury and Bridgwater Clubs kept the action going between them, while in the Wessex Centre it was still Minety Vale's circuit at Long Newnton which attracted the leading riders as well as some big crowds. The club certainly knew how to pump up the publicity, stating in their press advert 'Make your rendezvous the Mecca of the stars'.

Ten thousand spectators turned out in May for the Newnton Laurels, and it was that man John Gould who took the title from, in finishing order, Bill Bridgett, Jackie Sewell,

Ray Harris, Austin Cresswell, brother George Gould and Murray Briggs. The sidecar races were again won by 'Mr Long Newnton' Bill Evans, who was certainly the master at the Gloucestershire circuit as far as the chairs were concerned. Later on, in September, John Gould returned to the venue, and in a family one-two he won the Long Newnton Championship ahead of his sibling, with Lew Coffin in third spot.

Two other meetings took place in Gloucestershire as the revival of the sport started to take a grip all over the UK. At Dursley, Bill Bridgett won three finals, while both George Bewley and veteran Chris Boss enjoyed a victory apiece. The other event, run by the West Gloucs & Dean Forest Auto Club at Hurst Farm in Lydney, was witnessed by an audience of 2,500. Ron Taylor, Austin Cresswell and George Bewley were the solo stars on the day, while Ken Norcutt and partner Brian Peeling came out on top in the sidecars.

Going over the border to Herefordshire, there were various meetings during the year: Grafton Show, Ross Show, Much Marcle Show, Bosbury Show, Withington Show, Bullingham Show, Hereford Horse Show (at the racecourse) and the Ledbury Floral Fête. At Much Marcle, Austin Cresswell sped to the Challenge Cup, while at Withington it was the turn of Ray Harris to triumph. Meanwhile Ron Taylor cleaned up at Grafton, with Cresswell doing likewise at Hereford Racecourse. At Bullingham the honours were shared by George Bewley, Ray Harris, Ron Taylor and Bill Bridgett, and at the Ross Show there were three final successes for Harris, with a win apiece for Taylor and Cresswell. At Bosbury, Harris was again to the fore, although he was forced to share the honours with the brilliant Lew Coffin, who at last broke the monopoly that a handful of riders seemed to have on the region.

The Wye Valley Auto Club staged an October memorial for Charlie Jones. This wasn't the first time they had run such a meeting, as they had previously held similar events in memory of Ray Beaumont, both riders having lost their lives in racing accidents. Wellington was the venue, with Lew Coffin, Cyril Francis and Ray Harris being the solo winners, while Chris Vincent, Bill Evans and Ken Norcutt were the sidecar victors. Sadly the event was marred by another fatality in the fifth heat, when W. Littleford of Bilston succumbed to injuries sustained in a crash.

Staying in the Western Centre, the Three Counties Show took place at Malvern. This event ran from the 1950s to the end of the 1980s and was later revived by the Malvern Club in 2002. The 1959 running brought the following results:

> 350cc final – First: Austin Cresswell, Second: Jackie Sewell, Third: George
>   Bewley.
> 500cc final – First: Ray Harris, Second: George Sewell, Third: Ron Taylor.
> Unlimited final – First: Ray Harris, Second: Ron Taylor, Third: W. May.
> Challenge Cup final – First: Ray Harris, Second: Ron Taylor, Third: Jackie
>   Sewell.

In the Midlands area it was the Evesham and West Brom Clubs who kept the grass scene alive, with Ray Harris scooping the prestigious Worcestershire Championship. In Wales, action could be seen at Rhayader, Abergavenny, Presteigne, Builth Wells and Brecon, to mention a few venues. Austin Cresswell, Gerry Goodwin and Ray Harris tasted success in the Principality, with the latter covering himself in glory in the Welsh Championship.

It really was a splendid year for the sport in the North of England, with racing held at numerous places, including Clifton Park (Rotherham Club), Clitheroe Show (Ribble Valley Club), Kilburn (Thirsk Club), Kendal (Westmorland Club), Barnard Castle (Darlington Club), Otley Chevin (West Riding Club) and Rushyford (County Durham Club). Running through the solo riders who bossed the region, the list featured the likes of brothers Jack and Peter Fountain, Des Heckle, Maurice Wilkinson, Peter Houchin, Stan Tennent, Peter Wilson, Eric Atkinson, Peter Lloyd, Eric Carr, Ken Mellor and Paul Cross, while also appearing in the odd meeting was scrambler Arthur Lampkin. Turning to sidecars, the leading exponents were Roy Cunliffe, Dave Owen and Ken Whittaker, while just starting out in both the solos and the chairs was Mike Webster. Of course, Webster was later to become British Sidecar Champion, while son Steve went on to even greater things, becoming a multi World road-race sidecar winner during the 1980s, 1990s and on into the new millennium.

Scottish supporters were able to view the sport at various venues, including Arbroath, Stonehaven and Forfar, with the top riders being the Templeton brothers (Willie and Doug), Bill Landels and Andy Pryde. Meanwhile Robbie Allan, brother of future British Moto-Cross Champion Vic, was also doing well. These days Allan is better known for organizing the European Stunt Championship and the freestyle moto-cross exhibitions, while still competing in classic road-racing himself.

Looking at Ireland, on 6 January the Munster Motorcycle & Car Club acquired the massive Vernon Mount house and estate situated on the outskirts of Cork City. This not only became the club's headquarters, but racing was also held in the grounds. Meetings in Ireland were predominantly staged on the mountain-style circuits that had been plentiful in England before the war. Among others, the locations for racing included Terenure College grounds, Dublin; Butlin's holiday camp, Mosney; Drownleena Lawn, Dunmanway; Tassaggart; Kincoole; Birr; Fassaroe and Nenagh. Among many riders, those who featured prominently during the year were Gerry Scarlett, Mervyn Hayes, Harold Buchanan, Noel Bell and Eric Williams. One significant event occurred when the Motorcycle Union of Ireland decreed that competitors in grass-track or scrambles events would be required to wear protective clothing such as boots, gloves and an approved helmet, leaving one to wonder just how the riders had been kitted out in previous years!

1959 Roll of Honour

National Championships
350cc and 500cc – Alf Hagon
Sidecar – Freddie French/George Wasley
Inter-Centre Team (Solo) – East Midlands
Inter-Centre Team (Sidecar) –
South Midlands

Southern Centre Championships
250cc – Roger Adlam
350cc and Individual – John Gould
Sidecar – Mike Lane/Bill Woodward
Team – Blackmore Vale

South Midlands Centre Championships
125cc – Mike Gutsell
200cc – Ken Greer
250cc – Mike Griffiths
350cc and 1,000cc – Alf Hagon
Sidecar – Freddie French/George Wasley
Team – Southall

South-Eastern Centre Championships
200cc – Ted Stokes
250cc – Mick Philpott
350cc, 650cc and Unlimited – Don Godden
Sidecar – Freddie French/George Wasley

Eastern Centre Championships
250cc – Ted Ryman
350cc and 500cc – Alf Hagon
Sidecar – Derek Yorke/George Mason
Team – Tigers (Grays)

East Yorkshire Championship
Eric Carr

North Lancashire Championship
Ken Mellor

Worcestershire Championship
Ray Harris

Cambridgeshire Championship
Solo – Austin Cresswell
Sidecar – Ken Fisher/Bill Smith

Welsh Championship
Ray Harris

Fordham Trophy
350cc and 1,000cc – Austin Cresswell
Sidecar – Harold Hill

Loughborough Challenge Cup
Jackie Sewell

Carnival Kings Sidecar Cup
Bill Evans/Ron Jones

Long Newnton Championships
Solo – John Gould
Sidecar – Bill Evans/Ron Jones

Withington Show Challenge Trophy
Ray Harris

Much Marcle Show Challenge Cup
Austin Cresswell

Dave Bach Memorial Left-Hand Sidecar Trophy
Vernon Carr

Gunnell Trophy
Jimmy Rogers

Whittlesey Show Challenge Cup
Bill Bridgett

Bosbury Show Challenge Cup
Ray Harris & Lew Coffin (joint-first)

Grafton Show Challenge Cup
Ron Taylor

Somerset Challenge Shield
Ron Taylor

Long Newnton Laurels
Solo – John Gould
Sidecar – Bill Evans/Ron Jones

Ledbury Challenge Trophy
Ray Harris

Spalding Golden Helmet Final
Jackie Sewell

Willoughby Hedge Championships
350cc – Lew Coffin
500cc – Bill Bridgett
Novice – Eric Stroud
Sidecar – Bill Evans/Ron Jones

Bob Wilson Trophy
Arthur Stuffins

Clitheroe Show Challenge Cup
Eric Carr

Ken Smith Memorial Trophy
Don Godden

Charlie Jones Memorial
Lew Coffin

Ludlow Trophy
Bill Bridgett

Peterborough Show Challenge Cup
Bill Bridgett

Three Counties Show Challenge Cup
Ray Harris

Shapwick Challenge Trophy
Ron Taylor

Ross Show Challenge Trophy
Ray Harris

Don Davis Memorial Trophy
Eddie Bayley

Richmond Trophy
Jackie Sewell

Folkestone Championship
Don Godden

Barham Championship
Cyril Williams

Hereford Horse Show Challenge Cup
Austin Cresswell

Border Counties Show Challenge Cup
Ray Harris

11
GRASS-TRACK RACING
1960

As the 'Swinging Sixties' dawned, the National Championships moved to the Minety Vale Club's superb Long Newnton airfield circuit near Tetbury in the ACU Wessex Centre. Like the modern-day racing scene, spectators had arrived well in advance and camped out for the event of the year, with a huge race-day crowd estimated to be in the region of 15,000. Lew Coffin won the first heat of the meeting, a 350cc National team race, with subsequent victories following for Reg Luckhurst, George Bewley and Monty Banks in the same category.

Next it was the 500s, with the four winners being Austin Cresswell, Reg Luckhurst, George Bewley and Midlander Don Summers. Overall victory went to the power-packed Midlands outfit, which was represented by three of the aforementioned riders in Cresswell, Bewley and Summers, plus J.C. Annis. The sidecars followed, and the Southern Centre sped to the title, their team comprising Ken Norcutt, Mike Lane and I. Sims on his BSA. Looking at the individuals, the 350cc class featured heat victories for Alf Hagon, Don Godden and Lew Coffin. Having previously taken the title in 1954 and 1959, Hagon went on to complete a hat-trick of successes by daringly riding the outside line around the pack on the first turn to lead home from Godden, Denys Goodacre and Coffin.

Moving on to the 500cc class, Alf Hagon encountered mechanical gremlins in the heats, which resulted in victories for Ron Taylor, Austin Cresswell and Don Godden. The final then saw Cresswell clock the fastest time of the day to take victory – seven years after his last triumph in the category. Meanwhile George Gould enjoyed a good race to finish as runner-up ahead of Denys Goodacre and Godden.

Bearing in mind the history of the circuit, it is unlikely that many in the large audience would have bet against the sidecar master Bill Evans and his partner Ron Jones. They may have thought differently as the Tony Wakefield and Geoff Milton combination led over the opening lap. However, there was to be no upset as Evans and Jones came through to secure a fifth National title, having previously won in 1954, 1955, 1956 and 1957. Also in the thick of the action was Henry Body, with his brother Malcolm in the chair. They were mounted on a 650cc BSA machine, constructed by Jack Difazio, but sadly the track rod on the steering broke, causing the duo to pull up.

Top motorcycle announcer Peter Arnold was behind the microphone on the day, while clerk of the course and secretary for the meeting was leading speedway referee Cecil Telling. The officials also included three men from nearby Malmesbury, namely

A wheel-to-wheel duel at the 1960 National Championships featuring Reg Luckhurst (6) and Jackie Sewell (16).

Stan Curnock (club steward), Jack Griffith (chief marshal) and Dr Pym (track doctor). The main results of the day follow:

> 350cc final – First: Alf Hagon (Hagon JAP), Second: Don Godden (JAP), Third: Denys Goodacre (JAP), Fourth: Lew Coffin (LCS JAP), Fifth: Jackie Sewell (Twang Special).
> 500cc final – First: Austin Cresswell (JAP), Second: George Gould (JAP), Third: Denys Goodacre (JAP), Fourth: Ray Harris (JAP), Fifth: Don Godden (JAP).
> Sidecar final – First: Bill Evans/Ron Jones (Norton), Second: Tony Wakefield/Geoff Milton (Triumph), Third: Dave Nourish/Rob Williamson (WHB), Fourth: Ken Norcutt/Brian Peeling (BSA), Fifth: Roy Cunliffe/P. Wilson (Norton).
> Team Championship (Solo) – First: Midlands, Second: Southern, Equal Third: East Midlands, South-East and South Midlands.
> Team Championship (Sidecar) – First: Southern, Equal Second: East Midlands and Midlands, Fourth: Yorkshire, Fifth: East Yorkshire.

The event was a rip-roaring success, aided no end by the entry list, which read like a 'Who's Who' of the sport. Over thirty sidecar outfits participated, including future champions Mike Webster and Bryan Rust, plus previous victor Freddie French. The line-up also included several other drivers who were to make a name for themselves in their respective areas, including Ron Young (South-East), Dick Barton (Eastern), Graham Hancox (Midlands) and Henry Body (South-West). The solos included virtually all the top riders, with the notable exceptions being Martin Tatum and John Gould.

Of the other meetings staged at Long Newnton in 1960, one of the most prestigious was the Newnton Laurels. This was held in front of 13,000 good folk on 29 May, and with a £25 first prize up for grabs, it was hardly surprising that an all-star field was assembled. On the day, however, nobody could match the superb skills of John Gould from Fordingbridge, who took the title and the support finals. Along with Gould, there were heat victories for George Bewley, Don Godden and John Brickell, but it was Denys Goodacre and John's brother George, who followed him home in the big final.

The amazing Bill Evans and Ron Jones combination won both the sidecar Scratch finals, while John Gould was triumphant in the 350cc class, ahead of Don Godden and Tim Bungay. There was some consolation for Godden though, as he took the chequered flag in the Handicap race after John Gould had suffered a rare fall. There was a victory too for Reg Luckhurst in the Non-Winners category, ahead of Dave Nourish and Lew Coffin.

Some interesting names in the programme included Bruce Carter from Basingstoke, who many years later was to win the Southern Centre Championship and in recent times has been helping Andrew Appleton on the speedway scene; Ivor Lawrence, who was to become well known in the Midlands during the 1960s and 1970s; Gerry Wheeler from Somerset, who was a future British Sidecar Champion. Also listed was Polish speedway ace Tadeusz Teodorowicz, although in the event he was a non-starter. Affectionately known as 'Teo', he later sadly died following a track crash while riding for Swindon at West Ham in 1964.

The top three at the 1960 Long Newnton Laurels. From left to right: George Gould (41), Denys Goodacre (57) and John Gould (40).

Above: *Exciting
sidecar action from
the 1960 Long
Newnton Laurels as
Bill Evans (2) leads
Ken Fisher (49).*

Right: *The great Barry
Briggs (136) blasts
around the Lydden
circuit.*

The full result for the eight-lap Laurels final was: First: John Gould, Second: Denys Goodacre, Third: George Gould, Fourth: Austin Cresswell, Fifth: George Bewley, Sixth: Jackie Sewell, Seventh: John Brickell.

The year's South-Eastern Centre Championships were held at Folkestone Motorcycle Club's famous Rhodes Minnis circuit in Kent, and it was Don Godden who completed a marvellous triple by garnering the 350cc, 500cc and Individual titles. In the main Championship final he defeated Monty Banks, with Ted Jelf occupying third spot.

Alf Hagon was at his best to win the Sittingbourne Club's Redshaw Trophy ahead of Reg Luckhurst and Ted Jelf. At the same meeting Hagon also took victory in the Silver Helmet from Jelf, as well as emerging victorious in the 350cc final ahead of Luckhurst. Other action in the South-East saw the aforementioned Luckhurst in scintillating form at the Surrey Hills meeting in September, winning three finals. Previously, in August, at the Lydden-staged Barham Championship, speedway superstar Barry Briggs made an appearance, but it was not his day as Don Godden raced to a trio of successes.

Earlier in the season the Gould brothers, along with Tim Bungay and Lew Coffin, had paid a visit to the Astra Motorcycle Club's Lydden raceway. The Southerners did the business in the lightweight classes too, with Tim Bungay defeating Alf Hagon in the 250cc final while John Gould and Lew Coffin finished first and second respectively in the 350cc final, ahead of Don Godden. There was, however, revenge for both Hagon and Godden, as the former took victory in the Unlimited final, while the latter won the Championship final.

Needless to say, the top solo men in the South-East were Messrs Hagon and Godden, with many superb track battles taking place between the two over the course of the year. Although they were the leading duo in the area, there were a number of other solo stars who performed well including Reg Luckhurst, Ted Jelf, Monty Banks, Cyril Williams, Arthur Wicken, Ted Stokes, Sid Jarvis and Jack Colver. Aside from that impressive little list, a few new names also appeared in the results, namely Alan Angear, Tony Black and Pete Bonugli. Meanwhile, the Ron Young and Bob Penn combination proved to be top of the 'chairmen' in the section.

Turning to the Southern Centre, race meetings were run at Willoughby Hedge (Blackmore Vale Motorcycle Club), Ansty (Salisbury Club), Farnham Park (Farnham Club), the Mount (Ringwood Club), Westfield Farm (Totton Club), Mayles Farm (Totton Club), Wareham (Bournemouth Club), Kingsclere Road (Basingstoke Club), Dances Farm (Andover Club) and Corhampton Park (Bishop's Waltham Club), among others.

The Southern Centre Championships were staged at Willoughby Hedge and Lew Coffin was in dominant mood, taking both the 350cc and Individual titles, although Pete Munday did lead the star final only to be overwhelmed by Coffin. In the sidecars there was something of a surprise result as Ken Norcutt and Brian Peeling defeated multi-Champions Mike Lane and Sparrow Woodward to win their first title.

In September the Blackmore Vale Club again organized the popular Willoughby Hedge Championships, with Lew Coffin winning the 350cc event in the fastest time of the day, ahead of Tim Bungay and George Gould. In the 500cc final, Bungay led the field into the first turn, but within a lap Pete Munday was holding sway. In another positional

Lew Coffin (22) leads from the partially hidden Fred Parkins, Jimmy Gale (38), John Gould (40) and the rest of the field at the Mount, 1960.

Mike Lane (55) ahead of Ken Norcutt and John Callander at the Mount, 1960.

79

change George Gould moved ahead, and although it looked like the pressing Coffin would eventually overhaul his opponent, a nasty tumble saw his race end abruptly, leaving Gould to take the chequered flag in style. The major results of the meeting were:

> 350cc final – First: Lew Coffin (LCS), Second: Tim Bungay (LCS), Third: George Gould (JAP).
> 500cc final – First: George Gould (JAP), Second: Pete Munday (JAP), Third: Eric Stroud (JAP).
> Sidecar final – First: Bill Evans/Ron Jones (Norton), Second: Bob Keen/S. Scales (Triumph), Third: Henry Body/Malcolm Body (JD Special).

Briefly looking at some of the other events of the season in the area, Lew Coffin and George Gould were again the solo winners at Corhampton Park, with Bob Keen and Ken Norcutt collecting sidecar victories. The brilliant John Gould gleaned three successes at the Mount and repeated his performance at Bournemouth, where scrambler Dave Palmer also won a brace of finals. Another Corhampton Park meeting brought an amazing five final victories for George Gould, while at the same event Max Richards won the Novice event. Finally, at Basingstoke John Gould swept to a glorious double, winning the 350cc and 500cc finals prior to his brother George doing likewise at a later meeting.

Moving on to the South Midlands, and starting with the Centre Championships which were held on the kidney-shaped Chiltern Hills circuit at Stokenchurch, Alf Hagon raced to the 250cc and 350cc titles, and it looked as though he would wrap up the 500cc crown as well. However, as Doug Drewett challenged him, the double-victor hit a course-marking stake with his handlebar and was forced to retire, his throttle cable adjuster having broken off in the impact. That left Doug Drewett to go on and take the winning flag from John Argrave, with Eddie Bayley finishing in third position.

There was a large entry for the meeting, with the solo field including the likes of Arthur and Colin Sweby, Jimmy Rogers (the track record holder), Ken Greer, Alf Goodey and three riders at the beginning of their careers in Dave Kirby, Andy Ross and Barry Meeks. The Championship's results looked like this:

> 250cc final – First: Alf Hagon (Hagon JAP), Second: Don Baxter (Vixen), Third: B. Dulieu (Rees Special).
> 350cc final – First: Alf Hagon (Hagon JAP), Second: Jimmy Rogers (NEB Special), Third: Eddie Bayley (JAP).
> 500cc final – First: Doug Drewett (JAP), Second: John Argrave (JDA Special), Third: Eddie Bayley (JAP).
> Sidecar final – First: Bob Keen/S. Scales (Triumph), Second: John Browne/ G. Redding (JAP), Third: J. Walker/B. Fowler (BSA).

Looking at some of the other areas, Dave Nourish was a multi-final winner at the Diss Club's Brome Park in Suffolk, while Arthur Stuffins was a victor at the Maldon-staged

ESSA promotion in Essex. At Stockton-on-Tees, future sidecar Champion Mike Webster won two solo finals in the 250cc and 350cc classes, while Eric Carr took both the 500cc and Unlimited finals. In Yorkshire, Eric Carr was also successful at the Craven Club's Malham meeting, while the leading sidecar exponent in the area at many events was Roy Cunliffe on his super-quick Norton.

Remaining in the North of England, among others venues utilized during the year were Wolsingham, County Durham; Iveston, County Durham; Clifton Park, Rotherham; Thornton Road, Pickering; Apperley Bridge, Bradford and the Railway Athletic Sports Ground, Wetherby. There were also grass-track events staged at the Kilburn Feast in Thirsk, the Weardale Show and at Bainbridge Sports Show. The top riders in the area included the previously mentioned Eric Carr from Skipton, as well as Maurice Wilkinson (Kettlewell), Paul Cross (Goole), Des Heckle (Durham) and Peter Lloyd (Yarm).

Racing returned to Edgeley Park, Whitchurch in the Cheshire Centre, where the action was fast and furious as regular locals Jack Grindley and Keith Terretta battled with some of the national aces, plus scrambler Terry Challinor on his DOT machine.

In Lincolnshire, Oakham's Jackie Sewell raced to victories on his Twang Specials at Sleaford, with Joey Neath doing the same in the sidecars. Alf Hagon also visited Lincolnshire, winning a 250cc final at Boston ahead of Arthur Stuffins and Dave Nourish, but in the larger classes he had to give second best to the ace East Midlands trio of Stuffins, Arthur Pell and Denys Goodacre. Meanwhile future British Sidecar Champion Bryan Rust was starting to win in the area, as he showed at Boston with a double victory. At Loughborough the 'King' was Goodacre, who took the Unlimited Solo Challenge Cup for achieving the best results over the course of the season. The result was: First, Denys Goodacre 20 points; Second, Jackie Sewell 15; Third, Arthur Pell 7; Fourth, Dave Nourish 6; Fifth, Austin Cresswell 3.

One rather interesting event was held at Ipswich Speedway for grass-trackers and scramblers, entitled the 'East Anglian Short Circuit Championship'. This unfortunately took place amid heavy rainfall, with the results as follows:

Solos – First: Dave Nourish (WHB), Second: Andy Lee (BSA), Third: Tim
    Bungay (JAP).
Sidecars – First: P. Newman (Norton), Second: Oily Wells (JAP), Third: D. Bass
    (Norton).

The Cambridgeshire Championships were organized by Cambridge Centaur Motorcycle Club at St Ives, and Denys Goodacre followed up his 1958 and 1959 successes to retain the title, with Alf Hagon and Arthur Stuffins filling the other podium positions. Hagon also made trips up to the area to race at Sutton and Littleport, both of which were run by the Ely & District Motorcycle and Light Car Club. Hagon proved to be unstoppable at the latter venue, where his main opposition was provided by scrambler Andy Lee. At Sutton, Hagon collected another three final victories, although he had to accept defeat at the hands of Goodacre in the 350cc class.

The Ilford Amateur Club were still racing at Skinners Farm, Abridge in Essex, and in their July meeting, Kent's Sid Jarvis made his visit to the Eastern Centre worthwhile

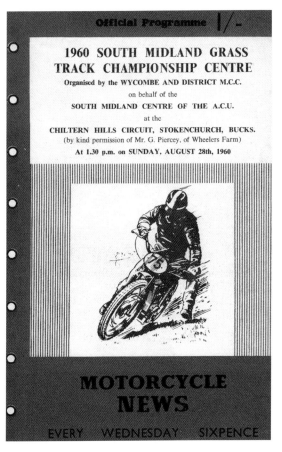

with two final wins over Arthur Wicken. He wasn't so fortunate in the Up to 1,000cc final category, however, as he finished as runner-up to Alf Goodey.

The East Midlands and Eastern Centres certainly dished up some excitement during 1960 with a multitude of events for both competitors and spectators to choose from. Aside from the ones previously covered, a seemingly endless list included other meetings at Woodnook (Grantham Club), Long Sutton (Peterborough Club), Melton (Rendlesham Club), Merton (Watton Club), the Wong Circuit, Horncastle (Banovallum Club), Holestone Moor (Derwent Club), Clay Lake Field (Spalding Club), Hykeham (Lincoln Club) and Scredington (Sleaford Club), as well as many different showground venues.

In the South-West, the Broadhembury and Bridgwater Clubs kept the flag flying, with the former hosting Saturday evening events at Greenham, near Wellington. Lew Coffin was the dominant rider at the venue in July, but the following month he only managed to triumph in the 350cc class, with Ron Heal, Adrian Kessell and future Exeter Speedway teamster Francis Cann winning the other finals. Meanwhile in the sidecars, Mike Lane, Ken Norcutt, John Callander and Viv Debben all took victories at these meetings.

Alf Hagon (255), Arthur Pell (98), Denys Goodacre (57), Ken Greer (116) and Arthur Stuffins (2) enter the first bend at Boston, 1960.

East Midlands greats Arthur Stuffins (2) and Arthur Pell (98) in the midst of battle.

The Bridgwater Club also ran two meetings, the first of which took place on Easter Monday at Shapwick. Lew Coffin again showed good form to defeat Adrian Kessell and Frank Evans, thereby scooping the Shapwick Challenge Trophy. Coffin made it a glorious treble by taking the 350cc and Open finals, while Shaftesbury's John Brickell won the second of the Open finals. Among those on show, the line-up of riders also included the likes of Chris Julian, Eric Roberts and Reg Hawken. Turning to the sidecar boys, four finals were held, and the results were certainly spread across the board with a win apiece for Ken Norcutt, John Callander, Viv Debben and I. Sims. A crowd of 2,000 watched Coffin triumph in the Somerset Challenge Shield later in July, again at Shapwick, with Kessell and Evans again having to settle for the minor rostrum positions behind.

The West Gloucester & Dean Forest Auto Club ran at Lydney, with a family double act doing the business in the 250cc final as Selwyn Perry took first place from brother Tig, both of them mounted on their Cotton scramblers. Proving it was no fluke the Perry boys also filled the first two positions in the Standard Machines final, and from then on the Perry name was to be synonymous with grass-track racing for the next forty years. The redoubtable Lew Coffin collected another three wins on the 500-yard Gloucestershire oval, but it was Tim Bungay who took victory in the 6-Fastest Handicap final, while Kidderminster's Ivor Lawrence won the Non-Winners final. In the sidecars there were final successes for John Browne, Ken Norcutt and John Short, whose son Gerald would later be a solo star in both grass-track and speedway. The meeting had a top-notch field, as emphasized by the solo field which also included Roger Elmore, Fred Powell, Austin Cresswell, Don Summers, Mike Watkins and Ron Heal.

Over the border in Herefordshire, the Western Centre showgrounds were in full flight, with the annual grass-track events taking place at Bosbury, Much Marcle, Bullingham, Hereford, Withington and Ledbury. The top aces at these meetings were Lew Coffin, Austin Cresswell, Ron Taylor, Bill Bridgett, Arthur Stuffins and George Bewley, with the likes of Ray Harris, Mike Wilmore, Tim Bungay, Trevor Plant and Cyril Francis also in the melting pot and challenging for honours.

In Ireland, racing went ahead in various places including Vernon Mount, Donaghadee, Kilvoole, Newcastle, Tallaght, Carrowdore and Clonmel. Meanwhile the Tara Motorcycle Club held their first meeting at Kilmoon, near Ashbourne in County Meath, with Gerry Scarlett emerging as the major winner. Aside from Scarlett, some of the other leading riders in Ireland during the season were Mervyn McConkey, Noel Bell, Mervyn Hayes and Tommy Robb.

Scotland saw action too, including meetings at Woodlands Farm, Ceres, near Cupar in Fife, and also at Forfar. At the former venue Robbie Allan took victory in the 350cc class, while Andy Pryde mopped up in three events, taking victory in the 500cc, Unlimited and Fastest Riders' finals. Future Scottish Champion Andy Pryde also found the winning formula at Forfar, taking the 250cc final.

There was also some racing in Wales at the Abergavenny and Border Counties Show, as well as at both Presteigne and Felindre.

1960 Roll of Honour

National Championships
350cc – Alf Hagon
500cc – Austin Cresswell
Sidecar – Bill Evans/Ron Jones
Inter-Centre Team (Solo) – Midlands
Inter-Centre Team (Sidecar) – Southern

Southern Centre Championships
250cc – Dickie Dale
350cc and Individual – Lew Coffin
Sidecar – Ken Norcutt/Brian Peeling
Team – Blackmore Vale

South Midlands Centre Championships
125cc – Jim Collins
200cc – K. Smith
250cc and 350cc – Alf Hagon
500cc – Doug Drewett
Sidecar – Bob Keen/S. Scales

South-Eastern Centre Championships
200cc – Arthur Wicken
250cc – Ray Whitling
350cc, 500cc and Individual – Don Godden
Sidecar – Ron Young/Bob Penn

Eastern Centre Championships
250cc, 350cc and 1,000cc – Alf Hagon
Sidecar – Derek Yorke/George Mason
Team – ESSA

East Yorkshire Centre Championships
Solo and Sidecar – Mike Webster

East Midlands Centre Team Championship
Loughborough

Worcestershire Championship
Austin Cresswell

Cambridgeshire Championships
Solo – Denys Goodacre
Sidecar – Bryan Rust/Dave Heath

Fordham Trophy
350cc and 1,000cc – Denys Goodacre
Sidecar – Johnny Warren/G. Hall

Loughborough Challenge Cup
Denys Goodacre

Carnival Kings Sidecar Cup
Bill Evans/Ron Jones

Long Newnton Laurels
John Gould

Withington Show Challenge Trophy
Arthur Stuffins

Much Marcle Show Challenge Cup
Arthur Stuffins

Whittlesey Show Challenge Cup
350cc – Jackie Sewell
500cc and Unlimited – Denys Goodacre

Bosbury Show Challenge Cup
Lew Coffin

Bullingham Show Challenge Cup
Austin Cresswell

Hereford Horse Show Challenge Cup
Ron Taylor

Ely Show Championships
350cc – Jackie Sewell
1,000cc – Denys Goodacre

Rendlesham Sidecar Grand National
Dave Nourish

CTS Trophy
Arthur Stuffins

Long Sutton Show
350cc – Jackie Sewell
500cc – Norman 'Rocky' Bailey
Unlimited – Doug Rolph

Ludlow Trophy
Alf Hagon

Don Davis Memorial Trophy
Jack Colver

Felindre Show Challenge Cup
Austin Cresswell

**Huntingdonshire County Show
Challenge Cup**
Solo – Denys Goodacre
Sidecar – Roy Caborn/Ken Wilkinson

Terry Small Cup
George Gould

Somerset Challenge Shield
Lew Coffin

Spalding Golden Helmet Final
Jackie Sewell

Redshaw Trophy
Alf Hagon

Dale Challenge Sidecar Trophy
Bryan Rust/Dave Heath

Lydney Motorcycle Trophy
Lew Coffin

Willoughby Hedge Championships
350cc – Lew Coffin
500cc – George Gould
Sidecar – Bill Evans/Ron Jones

Peterborough Show
250cc – Alf Hagon
350cc – Arthur Pell
500cc and Unlimited – Arthur Stuffins
Sidecar – Bill Evans/Ron Jones

Three Counties Show Challenge Cup
Ray Harris

Shapwick Challenge Trophy
Lew Coffin

Richmond Trophy
Jackie Sewell

12
GRASS-TRACK RACING
1961

The date for the year's number one event was 3 September as the National Championships moved from one famous circuit in 1960 to another at Chiltern Hills, Stokenchurch in Buckinghamshire. Organized by the Wycombe & District Club, the team races started the day's programme, with Alf Hagon defeating Don Godden and Reg Luckhurst in the opening 350cc race. There were certainly fireworks in the second race in that category as Denys Goodacre went right through the field after a bad start to beat John Argrave and Midlander Gerry Goodwin.

That was to set the trend for the day, with both Alf Hagon and Denys Goodacre later featuring strongly in the major solo titles. Indeed, following a fast getaway, the individual 350cc final brought a comfortable third successive victory for Hagon, with

The brilliant sidecar combination of Bryan Rust and Dave Heath (73).

Goodacre having to settle for the runner-up spot. It was a different story in the 500cc class, however, with Hagon having to fight his way through the field to finish fourth, while up front, Goodacre took the chequered flag after passing Austin Cresswell.

In the sidecar final there was a terrific battle between Southern ace Ken Norcutt and multi-Champion Bill Evans. Both outfits led at different stages in an exciting wheel-to-wheel scrap before the amazing Evans grabbed his sixth National success on the line, this despite not being partnered by chair colleague of old Ron Jones. Instead, Ian Paskin proved to be an excellent passenger.

The event attracted a star-studded line-up, and aside from those already mentioned, other leading sidecar drivers included Keith Blaynee, John Warren, Dave Nourish, Nigel Mead, John Shears, Roy Cunliffe, John Browne and Bryan Rust. Meanwhile the illustrious list of solo entries also featured Jon Erskine, Tim Bungay, Alf Goodey, Arne Hendriksen, Doug Rolph, Ray Bennett, Sid Jarvis, Norman Ruddle, Alan Angear, Don Godden, Pete Munday, Arthur Harris and Gerry Goodwin. The results from the big day were as follows:

> 350cc final – First: Alf Hagon, Second: Denys Goodacre, Third: Don Baxter, Fourth: Mike Hepworth, Fifth: Doug Drewett, Sixth: Jack Grindley.
>
> 500cc final – First: Denys Goodacre, Second: Austin Cresswell, Third: Doug Drewett, Fourth: Alf Hagon, Fifth: Jackie Sewell, Sixth: John Argrave.
>
> Sidecar final – First: Bill Evans/Ian Paskin, Second: Ken Norcutt/Brian Peeling, Third: Mike Lane/Bill Woodward, Fourth: Mike Webster/Dave Hunter, Fifth: John Short/T. Newman.
>
> Team Championship (Solo) – First: South-East, Second: East Midlands, Third: South Midlands.
>
> Team Championship (Sidecar) – First: Midlands, Second: East Yorkshire, Equal Third: Southern and Yorkshire.

There were two areas where grass-track racing was really starting to take off, and both were at opposite ends of the country too. The first was in Cornwall, where the sport had been sparse for several years. At Newquay a Wednesday night meeting was staged in July, when car racing was also included in the programme of events. In the solos the remarkable Adrian Kessell had an enjoyable time, taking victory in seven out of eight races, his only defeat being at the hands of scrambler Jack Holding in the second 250cc event.

Staying in the county, and in similar fashion to a number of the Western Centre events, the Royal Cornwall Show at Wadebridge included racing in the main arena as a grand finale. A mixture of grassers and scramblers participated in the event, run by the Pendennis Club, who had first organized racing in 1931. Ben Slee had a good day to emerge victorious in the 500cc final, ahead of Adrian Kessell and David Harvey, while Denzil Moyle was the winner in the sidecars.

The sport was also prospering up in Scotland, where meetings were held at Loch Leven, Stonehaven, Forfar, Montrose, Cupar and Dundee, as well as at the Grandview Stadium in Stevenston. Top riders north of the border were Andy Pryde, Robbie Allan, Willie Edwards, Bill Jardine and Bill Beattie, plus brothers Willie and Doug Templeton.

Devonian sidecar and solo great John Uglow (106) in full flight.

Several of the Scottish riders used scramble machines similar to those of the lads in Ireland. Mervyn Hayes, Eric Williams, John Barkley and Gerry Scarlett were the leading exponents on the Emerald Isle, with Hayes winning the 500cc Irish title at Butlin's holiday camp in Dublin. The Irish Southern Centre introduced a Star Championship and it was a memorable day for Gerry Scarlett, who scooped the 200cc, 250cc and 350cc titles, with Mervyn Hayes winning the 500cc final. Meanwhile, in September, for the first time, the sport was staged in front of 6,000 fans as part of the Rose of Tralee Festival at the town park, organized by the Dalcassian Motorcycle Club. Finally, in this brief look at the Irish scene, there was glory for a future grass-track ace from England, namely Dave Palmer, in the Munster Club's scrambles event.

There was plenty of action in Wales during the season, with Midlander Gerry Goodwin winning four finals at Lampeter, while Ron Taylor completed a hat-trick of victories at the Abergavenny and Borders Show. At the Easter Monday meeting at Builth Wells the selfsame Taylor enjoyed a brace of wins, although a new name appeared in the results with Cyril Jones taking the flag in the 250cc final. In May, West Country racer supreme Lew Coffin made the journey across to collect three final victories at the Watton, Brecon. At Presteigne, the finals were shared between Goodwin, Austin Cresswell and Don Summers, who took one win apiece, while Ray Harris notched up a

Above: *Concentration is the name of the game for Gerry Wheeler and R. Granville (81).*

Left: *Pete Munday was a top star on grass prior to taking up speedway, initially with Poole.*

double. Cresswell was again successful at Felindre with three wins, while Llandrindod Wells proved a happy hunting ground for solo racers Gerald Evans, Jack Grindley and that man Cresswell, with Alf Ellis claiming a sidecar double. Meanwhile, over on the West Coast at St Clears, near Carmarthen, there were a couple of victories for Brian Leaman, plus one for Ken Williams.

In the South-West of England, Jimmy Gale garnered a triple success when the Tiverton Club made a return to racing following a long break, while future British Champion Gerry Wheeler also took victory in a sidecar final. At Bridgwater, Lew Coffin retained the Somerset Challenge Shield, although Jon Erskine took a tumble when closely challenging, leaving Adrian Kessell and scrambler Arthur Harris to fill the minor podium positions.

In the Midlands, Austin Cresswell scooped a brace of victories, winning the 500cc and Unlimited finals at the Evesham Club's Saturday evening meeting, while Keith Blaynee was triumphant in both sidecar finals. Cresswell was very much the man to beat in the region as he was also successful in events organized by the Leamington and West Brom Clubs.

The Western Centre showgrounds were again a source of close, exciting racing due mainly to their small oval shapes. At the Three Counties Show the racing was run by the Malvern Club, with Ron Taylor taking the flag to win the main Challenge Cup final. The major results from the show were as follows:

350cc final – First: Austin Cresswell, Second: Lew Coffin, Third: John Argrave.
500cc final – First: Ray Harris, Second: Austin Cresswell, Third: Lew Coffin.
Challenge Cup final – First: Ron Taylor, Second: Austin Cresswell, Third: Lew Coffin.
6-Fastest final – First: Ron Taylor, Second: Lew Coffin, Third: Austin Cresswell.

At the Bosbury Show, grass-track action was organized by the Ledbury Club, with those present witnessing one success in a final apiece for Lew Coffin, Ron Taylor and Austin Cresswell. Meanwhile Tig Perry was victorious in the 250cc final for scrambles machines. A good line-up of regular winners, future stars and scramblers was assembled for this event, and aside from those previously named, other competitors included Brian Leaman, Trevor Plant, John Webb, Mick Burton, Fred Powell, Terry Sleeman, Mike Watkins and Bill Davies. Continuing with the theme, Taylor enjoyed more success when defeating Cresswell and Artie Harwood to lift the Withington Show Challenge Trophy in August.

Over in Gloucestershire, the Minety Vale Club again staged their Laurels event at Long Newnton. An all-star field battled for places in the eight-lap final on the 800-yard oval circuit, with the prize money on offer being: 1st £30, plus silver challenge trophy; 2nd £15; 3rd £10; 4th £5; 5th £2 10s; 6th £1 10s; 7th 15s, with all the other finishers receiving 10s. The previous year's meeting had seen the Gould brothers occupy first and third positions, while Denys Goodacre had provided the filling in between. However there was sure to be a complete change in 1961 as the Goulds had retired earlier in the season and Goodacre wasn't in the starting line-up. Those competitors present, however, did include Arne Hendriksen, Don Summers, George Bewley, Austin Cresswell, Stan Luck, Alf Goodey, Pete Munday, Norman Ruddle, Don Godden, Ray Harris, Reg Luckhurst, Alf Hagon, Ron Taylor, Ted Jelf and Jon Erskine, plus a trio of future Midlands aces in Ivor Lawrence, Colin Davenport and Peter Hall. Meanwhile, having his first taste of national-standard racing was local Malmesbury speedster John Stallworthy.

With the racing fast and furious, Alf Hagon, Don Godden and Austin Cresswell were each victorious in the three heats. The final then resulted in a win for Hagon from Godden and Cresswell, with Stan Luck, George Bewley and Alf Goodey following the meeting's main protagonists across the line in that order. Hagon's super-charged efforts also saw him claim victory in the 350cc, 500cc and team races, with the sidecar event going to the outstanding BSA-mounted duo of Ken Norcutt and Brian Peeling.

Another meeting was held at Long Newnton on 11 June, when Lew Coffin was in dominant mood, winning three finals. It was interesting to note, however, the finishing order in the second heat of the Unlimited event, as behind Coffin and the second-placed Pete Munday were local boys Ron Farr and John Stallworthy.

The South-Eastern Centre Championships were held by the GTSA (Grass-Track Sidecar Association) Club at Lower Halstow, and saw Peter Colver surge from the back to depose 200cc title holder Ray Whitling. The 250cc category was won by Ted Stokes, although he could be considered a tad fortunate since he shed a chain as he crossed the finish line! Reg Luckhurst proved to be the major player in the meeting, taking victory in the 350cc, 500cc and Unlimited finals, although he had to withstand particularly strong challenges from Alan Angear in the latter two. The full results from the meeting were:

> 200cc final – First: Peter Colver, Second: Ray Whitling, Third: M. Wise.
> 250cc final – First: Ted Stokes, Second: Ray Whitling, Third: W. Moran.
> 350cc final – First: Reg Luckhurst, Second: Alan Angear, Third: J. Denton.
> 500cc final – First: Reg Luckhurst, Second: Alan Angear, Third: Sid Jarvis.
> Unlimited final – First: Reg Luckhurst, Second: Alan Angear, Third: Sid Jarvis.
> Sidecar final – First: John Shears/Frank Shears, Second: Ron Young/Bob Penn,
>   Third: A. Smith/K. Balcombe..

Remaining in the South-East a prestigious annual event was launched, namely the Grand Slam, staged at Rhodes Minnis and organized by the Folkestone Club. The circuit, which had first been used in 1954, had a camber, down and uphill section and was particularly fast, with the track record going into the event held by Don Godden at 61.8mph. The solo and sidecar events resulted thus:

> Solo final – First: Reg Luckhurst, Second: Alf Hagon, Third: Don Godden.
> Sidecar final – First: Ron Young, Second: Frank Barwick, Third: John Shears.

There was further racing at Rhodes Minnis in June, when the leading aces from the area such as Alf Hagon, Don Godden and Arne Hendriksen had to contend with not only the then-double World Speedway Champion Barry Briggs, but also a future number one

NATIONAL
GRASS TRACK
CHAMPIONSHIP

Sunday 3 Sept. 1961 at 2 p.m.

CHILTERN HILLS CIRCUIT, STOCKENCHURCH, BUCKS.

ORGANISED BY : THE WYCOMBE
& DISTRICT M.C.C.

BY KIND PERMISSION
OF Mr. G. PIERCY
OF WHEELERS FARM

THE MOTOR CYCLE

YOUR FASTEST WAY TO THE FACTS · THURSDAY 9d.

Brothers Gordon and Ray Nunn – the dynamic sidecar duo.

at the 'shale game' in Bjorn Knutsson. The two speedway aces duly won their heats in the 350cc, 500cc and Championship events that followed, but it was Hagon who eventually reigned supreme by taking the chequered flag in all three finals. Knutsson did fill second position in both the 350cc and 500cc finals though, both times finishing ahead of Godden. Meanwhile, 'Briggo' had to be content with third spot in the Championship final behind runner-up Godden.

Alf Hagon prevailed in the South Midlands Centre Championships, held at Pedley Hill, between Hemel Hempstead and Dunstable. A top-class field featured the likes of Doug Drewett, Doug Rolfe, John Argrave and Don Baxter, but no one could match the flying Hagon, who won the 250cc, 350cc and 1,000cc titles. Looking at the sidecars, Bob Keen emerged as the winning driver, accompanied by S. Scales in the chair.

Other action in the South Midlands included a victory for Doug Drewett over John Argrave and Jim Collins in the Don Davis Trophy, staged at the Watford Club's Cassiobury Park. The same trio of racers were also in the thick of the action at other venues in the region, including events organized by both the Vampire and Hayes Clubs.

The Eastern and East Midlands areas were very strong hotbeds for the sport. At Skinners Farm, Abridge in the East, Ian Towns started to make his mark by recording a couple of runner-up finishes to Alf Goodey. In another meeting, for the Steed Trophy at Sudbury, Suffolk, Towns was a very creditable third, behind the victorious Alf Hagon and the second-placed Jack Hubbard. At Langford Maldon John Argrave's form was inspired as he grabbed three trophies at the Tony Radley Memorial meeting, run by the ESSA Club. Other results in the area saw Gethin Johnson defeat Arthur Stuffins and Doug Rolph to clinch the Nu-Texa Trophy at Lowestoft in May, while Denys Goodacre proved unbeatable at the Hunts Falcons Club's September meeting on the Godmanchester track.

In the East Midlands, spectators and competitors were spoilt for choice, with an abundance of events, including ones at Sleaford, Peterborough and Biggin, as well as plenty of showground racing. Other meetings, meanwhile, were held at Boston, Rushden (Overstone Park), Spalding (Clay Lake), Lincoln, Grantham (Woodnook) and Ely. Top solo riders in the region included Arthur Stuffins, Arthur Pell, Denys Goodacre, Ken Moss, Jackie Sewell and Ken Greer, while in the sidecars two of the leading drivers were Dave Nourish and Bryan Rust.

One event still taking place to this day is the Thursday afternoon end-of-summer grass-track meeting at Longnor in the Peak District. In 1961 it was Ken Moss who sped to victory in the Unlimited final, mounted on his 500cc Hagon-JAP.

In the North, meetings were organized by the Runcorn and Pickering Clubs, while the Houghton & Hatton Club ran at the Woodland Agricultural Show near Bishop Auckland, where Skipton's Eric Carr took victory in the up to 1,000cc class.

Later in the season Lew Coffin was again victorious in the Willoughby Hedge Championships (run by the Blackmore Vale Club), winning both the 350cc and Individual events, while Bill Evans and Ron Jones made the trip from the Midlands worthwhile by retaining the sidecar title. The meeting attracted an all-star field, with riders from Cornwall, the South Midlands, Wessex and the Western Centres taking on the Southern boys. Indeed, well-known names listed in the solo section of the programme included Doug Drewett, Adrian Kessell, Stan Formhalls, Pete Munday, Jimmy Gale, Norman Pike, Jon Erskine, Tom Albery, Richard May, Mike Watkins, Pete Swain, John Trevitt, John Stallworthy, Peter Randall and Austin Cresswell. The sidecars were also well represented with a whole host of top drivers on show such as Gordon Nunn, Henry Body, John Browne, John Callander, Viv Debben, Tony Donadel, Harry Bone and Jack Knight.

It is worth noting that John Gould rode in his last meeting at Willoughby Hedge on 16 April 1961, after receiving leg injuries in the Fastest-12 race at Andover on 17 July the previous year. In fact, both Gould brothers retired following the Willoughby Hedge event of 16 April.

Finally, looking at the Southern Centre, racing was held at various places, including Basingstoke, Salisbury, Ringwood, Andover, Waterlooville and Farnham. The regional Championships were organized by the Bishop's Waltham Club, and staged at Corhampton. Lew Coffin again took the 350cc and Individual Championship titles, with Blackmore Vale retaining their team shield. In another repeat performance, the pairing of Ken Norcutt and Brian Peeling took the sidecar honours, leaving Eric Stroud's 250cc victory as the only different success to the previous year.

1961 Roll of Honour

National Championships
350cc – Alf Hagon
500cc – Denys Goodacre
Sidecar – Bill Evans/Ian Paskin
Inter-Centre Team (Solo) – South-East
Inter-Centre Team (Sidecar) – Midlands

Southern Centre Championships
250cc – Eric Stroud
350cc and Individual – Lew Coffin
Sidecar – Ken Norcutt/Brian Peeling
Team – Blackmore Vale

South Midlands Centre Championships
125cc and 200cc – Mike Gutsell
250cc, 350cc and 1,000cc – Alf Hagon
Sidecar – Bob Keen

South-Eastern Centre Championships
200cc – Peter Colver
250cc – Ted Stokes
350cc, 500cc and Unlimited –
Reg Luckhurst
Sidecar – John Shears/Frank Shears

East Yorkshire Centre Championship
Arthur Stuffins

East Midland Centre Team Championship
Spalding & Tongue End

Irish Championships
250cc – Mervyn Hayes
350cc – Gerry Scarlett
500cc – Eric Williams

Worcestershire Championship
Austin Cresswell

Grand Slam
Solo – Reg Luckhurst
Sidecar – Ron Young/Bob Penn

Fordham Trophy
350cc and 1,000cc – Alf Hagon
Sidecar – Roy Caborn/Ken Wilkinson

Loughborough Challenge Cup
Denys Goodacre

Carnival Kings Sidecar Cup
John Warren/G. Hall

Long Newnton Laurels
Alf Hagon

Withington Show Challenge Trophy
Ron Taylor

Much Marcle Show Challenge Cup
Ron Taylor

Whittlesey Show Challenge Cup
250cc – Jackie Sewell
350cc – Arthur Stuffins
500cc and Unlimited – Arthur Pell
Sidecar – John Warren

Bosbury Show Challenge Cup
Ron Taylor

CTS Trophy
Arthur Stuffins

Long Sutton Show
250cc, 350cc and 500cc – Alf Hagon
Unlimited – Arthur Pell
Sidecar – Roy Caborn/Ken Wilkinson

Don Davis Memorial Trophy
Doug Drewett

Somerset Challenge Shield
Lew Coffin

Spalding Golden Helmet Final
Jackie Sewell

Willoughby Hedge Championships
Novice – Ray Lambourne
250cc – Eric Stroud
350cc and Individual – Lew Coffin
Sidecar – Bill Evans/Ron Jones

Three Counties Show Challenge Cup
Ron Taylor

Hopkins Silver Challenge Cup
Austin Cresswell

Bishop Bevan Cup
Ray Harris

Richmond Trophy
Denys Goodacre

Sleaford Championship
Denys Goodacre

Royal Cornwall Show Challenge Cup
Brian Slee

R.M. Wood Trophy
Brian Gladwell

Border Counties Show
350cc and 500cc – Ron Taylor
Unlimited – Ray Harris

Ludlow Trophy
Arthur Stuffins

Donald Stead Trophy
Alf Hagon

Crawley Championship
Alf Hagon

Folkestone Championship
Alf Hagon

Dave Bach Memorial Left-Hand Sidecar Trophy
Jack Shears

Runcorn Championship
Jack Grindley

Cornell Challenge Cup
Ted Ryman

Ashby Challenge Cup
Arthur Stuffins

Star Challenge Cup
John Argrave

Tony Radley Trophy
John Argrave

Nobby Clarke Challenge Cup
John Argrave

Hadler Challenge Sidecar Shield
H.W. Maslin/D. Wright

Essex Chronicle Sidecar Cup
Derek Yorke/George Mason

13
GRASS-TRACK RACING
1962

Grass-track supporters are well-versed in the part played by the Evesham Motorcycle Club in the history of the sport. In 1962 the famous club was rewarded by staging the National Championships at their Ham Dean Farm circuit near Pinvin in Worcestershire. The day belonged to Alf Hagon, who took victory in both the 350cc and 500cc categories, with Don Godden finishing as runner-up in each. However, representing the South-East, Godden did at least have the consolation of landing the team title, along with Alan Angear, Tony Black and Ted Jelf. Meanwhile the other major contest resulted in a sidecar triumph for the Bryan Rust/Dave Heath combination, which held off the Nunn's (Gordon and Ray) for a fine success. The day's results were as follows:

350cc final – First: Alf Hagon (Hagon), Second: Don Godden (JAP), Third: John Argrave (JAP), Fourth: Denys Goodacre (Hagon), Fifth: Dave Palmer (JAP), Sixth: Jim Collins (JAP).

500cc final – First: Alf Hagon (Hagon), Second: Don Godden (JAP), Third: Denys Goodacre (Hagon), Fourth: Doug Drewett (JAP), Fifth: Bill Bridgett (JAP), Sixth: Ted Jelf (JAP).

Sidecar final – First: Bryan Rust/Dave Heath (BSA), Second: Gordon Nunn/Ray Nunn (GRN JAP), Third: Roy Woodhouse/Dave Woodhouse (BSA), Fourth: Derek Yorke/George Mason (Tri-JAP), Fifth: Dave Nourish/Robin Williamson (WHB).

Team Championship (Solo) – First: South Midlands 48pts, Equal Second: South-East and East Midlands 34.

Team Championship (Sidecar) – First: East Midlands 17pts, Equal Second: Southern and South Midlands 15.

With a magical hat-trick of title wins (250cc, 350cc and 1,000cc), Alf Hagon was also the main man at the Eastern Centre Championships, held by the Ilford Club at Abridge. The results from the event were:

250cc final – First: Alf Hagon, Second: Brian Dulieu, Third: Denis McHarris.
350cc final – First: Alf Hagon, Second: Alf Goodey, Third: George Markey.
500cc final – First: Alf Hagon, Second: Alf Goodey, Third: Ian Towns.

Right: *Alf Hagon (59) on his way to a double success at the 1962 National Championships.*

Below: *Top drivers Derek Yorke (107) and Dave Nourish do battle at the National Championships, 1962.*

Sidecar final – First: Derek Yorke/George Mason, Second: P. Rumsey/P. Benfield, Third: A.R. Parker/E.J. Hardy.
Team – First: ESSA, Second: Ilford A, Third: Halstead.

Alf Hagon was a winner at other Eastern Centre events during the year, including the National ACU Star round at Maldon, where he raced to a double success in the 250cc and 500cc classes. With the racing organized by ESSA, the Essex Show at Great Leighs produced a different victor, however, when 'King of the Showgrounds' Arthur Stuffins sped to the chequered flag in the All-Comers 300-1,000cc final, as well as the Fastest Riders' event.

The remarkable Alf Hagon was pretty dominant during the season, and enjoyed much success in the South-East, another of his personal highlights being a victory in one of the Sittingbourne Club's prestigious Silver Helmet meetings. However, it wasn't Hagon's day when it came to one of the biggest events in the grass-track calendar, namely the Folkestone Grand Slam. It was obvious that Swedish speedway star Bjorn Knutsson was the quickest rider on show, but when it came to the final it was fellow Southampton Speedway representative Reg Luckhurst who retained the title he had won the previous year. Mounted on board his Fred Jarvis machine, Luckhurst raced home as his main challengers, Knutsson, Hagon and Don Godden, all dropped out. Meanwhile in the sidecars, the experienced combination of Dave Nourish and Rob Williamson took victory ahead of the Ray Gerring/Kevin McCullagh pairing. The official results follow:

Solo Grand Slam – First: Reg Luckhurst, Second: Tony Black, Third: Bill Bridgett, Fourth: Stan Luck.
Sidecar Grand Slam – First: Dave Nourish/Rob Williamson, Second: Ray Gerring/Kevin McCullagh, Third: Ken Norcutt/Brian Peeling.

Bjorn Knutsson did have the consolation of winning both the Solo and 650cc finals at the South-Eastern Centre Championships though, with other victories going to Ray Whitling (200cc), Alf Hagon (250cc) and Don Godden (350cc), while Ron Young and partner Bob Penn raced away to take the Sidecar final.

This was the year when television cameras were at a number of grass-track events, and in the South-East region they covered the Astra TV Trophy, which saw yet another success for Alf Hagon from Reg Luckhurst and Don Godden. The cameras were also in position to capture the action at the GTSA TV Trophy when Godden came home first, with Hagon and Dave Palmer filling the other two podium positions.

There was a feast of activity for fans in the South-East, with meetings every Sunday from March to October. Aside from the leading competitors already mentioned, folk were able to see the likes of Des Lukehurst, Peter Colver, Martin Tatum, Malcolm Simmons, Alan Angear, Dave Mitchell, Chris Stewart and Derek Andrews in the solos, while the sidecars included Ron Young and John Shears.

The television crew made another appearance at Manor Farm, Exton on 5 August to film a meeting run by the Bishop's Waltham Club. The Nunn's won the Sidecar Southern TV Trophy, while Lew Coffin cantered to victory from Dave Palmer in the solos. Interestingly co-author Dave Stallworthy's brother John fell in the third heat, while Maurice Croucher, son of the former Southern Centre Champion Bert, took a tumble in heat four. In what was a high-quality field, other top solo exponents at the meeting included Richard May (later of Reading Speedway fame), Jon Erskine, Pete Munday, John Argrave, Pete Swain and Stan Formhalls.

The Southern Centre Championships were held by the Ringwood Club at Blashford, with Lew Coffin gleaning three titles (250cc, 350cc and 1,000cc), while Ken Norcutt and Brian Peeling finished on top of the pile in the sidecar category. The same duo also won the Blackmore Vale Club's ACU Star round at Willoughby Hedge, with Don Godden (350cc) and that man Alf Hagon (500cc) taking solo victories.

There were events on most weekends in the area, and the top boys were predominantly Lew Coffin, Dave Palmer, Jon Erskine and Pete Munday, although the likes of Richard May, Fred Saunders, Colin Sweby, John Stallworthy and John Trevitt often proved well capable of 'mixing it' with the regular aces. Looking at the sidecars, Ken Norcutt had by this time taken over from Mike Lane as the leading driver in the region.

Up in the North there was a lot of racing to be seen at places like Gateshead, Skipton, Wolsingham, Cresswell (Northumberland), Bagby (North Yorkshire), Haslingden (Lancashire), Runcorn and Hazel Grove, near Stockport. Several meetings were of the showground type, one of which took place at the Bainbridge Sports Society Show in North Yorkshire, incorporating a scramble track and a hill climb. Scrambler Alan Lampkin dominated the event, while Mike Webster took the sidecar honours.

In the Midlands the West Brom, Evesham and Leamington Clubs all hosted race meetings, with the former also holding an ACU Star round which resulted in victories

Don Freemantle (65) strives to stay ahead of Lew Coffin (22) at Blashford, 1962.

A terrific start-line shot of sidecar action from a West Brom Club event.

for Austin Cresswell (350cc final) and Gerry Goodwin (500cc final), as well as Ken Norcutt and Brian Peeling (Sidecar final). The Evesham Club's annual Worcestershire Championship was won by local rider Dave Langston, with the event staged by the banks of the river at the picturesque Corporation Meadow, actually in the town of Evesham itself.

The East Midlands was certainly the Mecca for the sport, with racing each and every week, including the Fordham Trophy, staged near Newmarket and organized by the Ely & District Club. Grass-track activity was also seen at the Cambridgeshire Show in Chatteris and the Newark and Notts Show in Newark, plus the Long Sutton and Whittlesey Shows in Peterborough. Aside from those, supporters in the area could also view the action at Littleport, Skegness, Retford and Wisbech to name but a few of the venues. Filling the top positions with regularity in the region were solo stars Jackie Sewell, Brian Maxted, Arthur Stuffins, Denys Goodacre and Ken Moss, with the top sidecar drivers being Dave Nourish, Nigel Mead, Bryan Rust, Mick Adams and Mike Webster. Among the major victories in the area were Jackie Sewell's success in the

Richmond Trophy, Denys Goodacre's winning of the Ludlow Trophy at the Littleport Show and the Spalding & Tongue End Club's triumph in the East Midlands Centre Team Championship.

Turning to the South Midlands, the Watford & District Motorcycle Club were holding their race meetings at Pedley Hill near Hemel Hempstead, while the Vampires Motorcycle Club ran at Potters Bar. The Stevenage Motorcycle Club were also staging meetings in the region, which was largely dominated by the likes of John Argrave, Alf Goodey, Jim Collins, Doug Rolph and Doug Drewett, with youngster Colin Sweby collecting some final victories too. The Watford Club started to run regular 'vintage races' in their programme of events, with 'Dinger' Bell and Willie Willshire winning several of the solo finals, while Freddie French and Ray Gerring did likewise in the sidecar categories.

In the Wessex Centre it was the Minety Vale Club's last major grass-track year, and their big meeting at Long Newton was the ACU Star round/Alma Cogan Trophy. Unfortunately, several top riders like Lew Coffin were absent for the event as it clashed with a meeting at Salisbury. A message from female vocalist Alma Cogan appeared in the race-day programme, and it was National Champion Alf Hagon who picked up the

trophy when he defeated Don Godden in front of an estimated 6,000 crowd. Full results from the meeting on the 700 yard circuit were as follows:

350cc ACU Star round – First: Alf Hagon, Second: Denys Goodacre, Third: Don Godden.

350cc Scratch final – First: Alf Hagon, Second: Denys Goodacre, Third: Don Godden.

500cc ACU Star round – First: Don Godden, Second: Alf Hagon, Third: Fred Powell.

500cc Scratch final – First: Alf Hagon, Second: George Bewley, Third: Don Godden.

Alma Cogan Trophy – First: Alf Hagon, Second: Don Godden, Third: George Bewley.

Sidecar ACU Star round – First: Ken Norcutt/Brian Peeling, Second: Mike Webster/Dave Hunter, Third: John Browne/Les Redding.

Sidecar Up to 1,200cc final – First: Ken Norcutt/Brian Peeling, Second: Mike Webster/Dave Hunter, Third: Tony Donadel/Ian Bird.

Carterton's John Browne was in his last season of racing, and having started way back in 1927, his third-place finish in the ACU Star round could be considered a great result amid such quality company. In the solo racing, top trials rider Peter Stirland and scrambler Ken Messenger were among those taking part, along with a young Pat Wiggins from Swindon.

The Wilts Border Club came up with an excellent track at Chiverlins Farm, Derriads, near Chippenham, with a good line-up of riders assembled to tackle the 500-yard circuit, including Glyn Chandler, Frank Evans and George Bewley. The latter named speedster from Pershore, who was famous for the Bewley frame and carburettor, raced to no less than four final victories, although he had to give second best to Chandler in the Up to 1,000cc Open final. Other riders who fared well in the meeting included Hereford's Mike Watkins, Tig Perry from Gloucestershire, all-rounder Dave Langston (who had earlier in the season lifted the Worcestershire Championship aloft) and the spectacular Trevor Plant.

Andy Pryde was still the man to beat in Scotland, while in Ireland the leading riders were Gerry Scarlett, Eric Williams, Mervyn Hayes and Jack Agnew. At the Dublin & District Club's circuit at Butlin's in Mosney, the latter named Agnew (mounted on a JAP) won the Irish 2-Mile 350cc Championship, while also posting the fastest time of the day.

In Wales, the Rhayader Club held their annual Whit Monday meeting, with Shropshire's Jack Grindley taking the honours for a third time. Lew Coffin made the journey to Brecon to win the 350cc, 500cc and Unlimited finals at the Welsh Championships, with Ron Taylor twice finishing as runner-up. Meanwhile Gerry Goodwin emerged triumphant from the 250cc final, ahead of Tig Perry. At Presteigne the spoils of success were shared, with Selwyn Perry, Ron Taylor and Gerry Goodwin collecting a win apiece, while Austin Cresswell scooped a brace of victories. Down at Carmarthen Park, Coffin again plundered a bootful of trophies, while Goodwin took the 250cc final.

Carterton's John Browne (34) heads Viv Debben (30) at a Blackmore Vale meeting, 1962.

Staying in the Principality, Gerry Goodwin showed a liking to the track at Llanbister, completing a golden treble before losing out to Ron Taylor in the Unlimited final. Sidecars were included in the programme at this venue, with wins claimed by both Ivor Lawrence and Roy Woodhouse. The Penybont Racecourse at Llandrindod Wells saw Cyril Jones win three finals, while at Abergavenny the annual show featured a victory each for Tig Perry, Dave Langston, Ron Taylor and Norman Storer – the latter a future speedway teamster at Long Eaton and Leicester.

The South-Western Centre was starting to gain momentum, with the main clubs organizing race meetings being Broadhembury, Otter Vale, Yeo Vale (Yeovil), South Molton and Tiverton. The star solo rider in the region was Lew Coffin, although he received stern opposition from Adrian Kessell and Bideford's Peter Jeffery, the father of future racing brothers Peter and Paul. On the sidecar front the leading drivers proved to be Gerry Wheeler, Gordon Gill, Trevor Stuckey and John Uglow. Plenty of visitors did well in the area during the year, the ones particularly of note being Dave Langston, Bill Davies, Jimmy Gale and Fred Saunders.

The Broadhembury & District Motorcycle Club ran a meeting at Gamlin's Farm, Greenham, near Wellington on Whit Sunday 10 June, and the event proved very popular as emphasized by a line-up of riders ranging from the Midlands down to Cornwall. Glancing at some of the more well-known faces, the list included men such as Ray Lambourne (from Farnham), Trevor Plant (Coleford), John Trevitt (Parkstone), Tom Albery (Gosport), Jon Erskine (Romsey), Bob Hughes (Bath), Stan Formhalls

(Southampton), Pete Munday (Totton), Pete Swain (Parkstone), Don Freemantle (Swanwick), Artie Thick (Eastleigh), Tig and Selwyn Perry (Gloucester) and John Stallworthy (Malmesbury). The sidecar brigade had to contend with some quality visiting drivers too, namely Jack Knight (Eastleigh), Ray Gerring (Oxford), Harry Bone (Southampton), Ken Norcutt (Reading), Cecil Taylor (Totton), Viv Debben (Ringwood), John O'Keefe (Bristol) and Tony Donadel (Bristol).

Looking at the Western Centre, the major events were the various popular show-ground meetings, and the results from some of these were as follows:

Three Counties Show, Malvern
350cc final – First: Lew Coffin, Second: Ron Taylor, Third: Austin Cresswell.
500cc final – First: Lew Coffin, Second: Austin Cresswell, Third: Bill Bridgett.
Challenge Cup – First: Lew Coffin, Second: Bill Bridgett, Third: George Bewley.
Unlimited final – First: Lew Coffin, Second: Bill Bridgett, Third: Austin
     Cresswell.
6-Fastest final – First: Bill Bridgett, Second: Lew Coffin, Third: Austin Cresswell.

Withington Show
350cc final – First: Ron Taylor, Second: Arthur Stuffins, Third: Dave Langston.
500cc final – First: Ron Taylor, Second: Mike Watkins, Third: Arthur Stuffins.
Challenge Cup – First: Lew Coffin, Second: Ron Taylor, Third: Arthur Stuffins.
Unlimited final – First: Lew Coffin, Second: Ron Taylor, Third: Arthur Stuffins.
8-Fastest Handicap final – First: Peter Hall, Second: Selwyn Perry, Third: Trevor
     Plant.

Worcester International Motoball Match Closing Event
250cc final – First: Tig Perry, Second: Arthur Stuffins, Third: Peter Hall.
350cc final – First: Arthur Stuffins, Second: Ron Taylor, Third: C. Smith.
500cc final – First: Ron Taylor, Second: Mike Watkins, Third: Arthur Stuffins.
Unlimited final – First: Ron Taylor, Second: Mike Watkins, Third: Arthur Stuffins.

Much Marcle Show
500cc final – First: Ron Taylor, Second: Ray Harris, Third: Mike Watkins.
Challenge Cup – First: Ray Harris, Second: Ron Taylor, Third: Mike Watkins.
Unlimited final – First: Ron Taylor, Second: Ray Harris, Third: Mike Watkins.
6-Fastest Handicap final – First: Cyril Jones, Second: F. Thompson, Third: Ron
     Taylor.

Mountain grass-track events were also staged by the West Dean and Ross-on-Wye Clubs. At Howle Hill, run by the Ross Club, top scramblers took on and defeated some of the grass boys, with Chris Horsfield, Mick Burton, Malcolm Davis, Billy Jackson and Jim Timms all featuring highly in the results against the likes of Gerry Goodwin and Selwyn Perry. Amazingly, forty years on, Gloucester's Jim Timms was still involved in racing, but of the four-wheel variety!

1962 Roll of Honour

National Championships
350cc and 500cc – Alf Hagon
Sidecar – Bryan Rust/Dave Heath
Inter-Centre Team (Solo) – South Midlands
Inter-Centre Team (Sidecar) – East Midlands

National ACU Star Championships
350cc – Don Godden
500cc – Alf Hagon
Sidecar – Ken Norcutt/Brian Peeling

Southern Centre Championships
250cc, 350cc and Individual – Lew Coffin
Sidecar – Ken Norcutt/Brian Peeling
Team – Blackmore Vale and
Bishop's Waltham (joint-first)

South Midlands Centre Championships
125cc – Mike Gutsell
200cc – Jim Collins
250cc and 350cc – John Argrave
500cc – Doug Drewett
Sidecar – John Shears/Frank Shears
Team – Southall

South-Eastern Centre Championships
200cc – Ray Whitling
250cc – Alf Hagon
350cc – Don Godden
650cc and Individual – Bjorn Knutsson
Sidecar – Ron Young/Bob Penn

Eastern Centre Championships
250cc, 350cc and 1,000cc – Alf Hagon
Sidecar – Derek Yorke/George Mason
Team – ESSA

East Yorkshire Champion
George Chapman

East Midlands Centre Team Championship
Spalding & Tongue End

Worcestershire Championship
Dave Langston

Grand Slam
Solo – Reg Luckhurst
Sidecar – Dave Nourish/Rob Williamson

Fordham Trophy
350cc and 1,000cc – Denys Goodacre
Sidecar – Bryan Rust/Dave Heath

Loughborough Challenge Cup
Denys Goodacre

Carnival Kings Sidecar Cup
Keith Blaynee/G. Sanders

Withington Show Challenge Trophy
Lew Coffin

Much Marcle Show Challenge Cup
Ray Harris

Whittlesey Show Challenge Cup
250cc – Dave Nourish
350cc and 500cc – Arthur Stuffins
Unlimited – Jackie Sewell

Long Sutton Show
350cc and 500cc – Arthur Stuffins
Unlimited – Gerry Goodwin
Sidecar – Bryan Rust/Dave Heath

Don Davis Memorial Trophy
Alan Chambers

Spalding Golden Helmet Final
Arthur Stuffins

Three Counties Show Challenge Cup
Lew Coffin

Richmond Trophy
Jackie Sewell

Sleaford Championship
Denys Goodacre

Ludlow Trophy
Denys Goodacre

Bedford Cup
Ken Norcutt/Brian Peeling

Dave Bach Memorial Left-Hand Sidecar Trophy
John Shears/Frank Shears

Runcorn Championship
Don Summers

Alma Cogan Trophy
Alf Hagon

Astra TV Trophy
Solo – Alf Hagon
Sidecar – Sid Martin

Ely Show
350cc and 1,000cc – Bill Bridgett

Essex Show
Solo – Arthur Stuffins
Sidecar – Derek Yorke/George Mason

Peterborough Show
350cc – John Argrave
500cc – Arthur Stuffins
Unlimited – Barry Briggs

Newark & Notts Show
250cc and 500cc – Denys Goodacre
Unlimited – Arthur Stuffins

Coventry Cathedral Championships
Solo – Arthur Stuffins
Sidecar – Keith Blaynee/G. Sanders

Bishop's Waltham TV Trophy
Solo – Lew Coffin
Sidecar – Gordon Nunn/Ray Nunn

GTSA TV Trophy
Solo – Don Godden
Sidecar – Ron Young/Bob Penn

Somerset Championships
Solo – Lew Coffin
Sidecar – Ray Gerring/Kevin McCullagh

14
GRASS-TRACK RACING
1963

The National Championships moved to another popular circuit for 1963, with the event, organized by the Folkestone Motorcycle Club, taking place at Rhodes Minnis in Kent. It proved to be a fabulous meeting, with riders coming from the back to win all three individual titles. The 350cc final was contested by a marvellous array of talent in George Markey, Jackie Sewell, Stan Luck, Denys Goodacre, Alan Angear, Gerry Goodwin, Malcolm Simmons, Alf Hagon, Don Godden, Fred Blower and Dave Palmer. The race was a good one, which finally saw Alf Hagon take advantage to win when Godden missed a gear, with regular contender Goodacre also making the most of the opportunity to snatch second spot.

The list of riders who made it through to the final of the 500cc category was probably even more impressive and read thus: Reg Luckhurst, Ivor Lawrence, George Bewley, Colin Sweby, Bill Bridgett, George Markey, Alan Angear, Malcolm Simmons, Alf Hagon, Don Godden, Denys Goodacre and Gerry Goodwin. Riding on home turf, the race eventually went to Luckhurst who came through following a battle with Bridgett, prior to passing Hagon on the inside for a fine victory.

Looking at the sidecars, another top-notch field made it through to the final, namely Ken Norcutt/Brian Peeling, Nigel Mead/Dave Hunter, Mike Webster/John Justice, Derek Yorke/George Mason, John Sykes/Dave Reynolds, Bryan Rust/Dave Heath, Dave Nourish/J. Curtis plus Ron MacBeth/Norman Wager. In what was a cracking exhibition of racing, the defining moment saw the Yorkshire combination of Mead and Hunter overhaul the Rust and Heath pairing to triumph.

Turning to the team events, the South-East wrapped up the solo contest, their side consisting of Don Godden, Reg Luckhurst, Stan Luck, Malcolm Simmons and Alan Angear. Meanwhile, with a team made up of Bryan Rust/Dave Heath, Dave Nourish/J. Curtis and Mick Adams/Brian Munday, the East Midlands emerged victorious in the sidecar competition.

To cap an exciting meeting on what was undoubtedly one of the world's leading circuits, all the trophies were presented by former Midland grass-track ace and 1960s sidecar road-racer Bill Boddice. Little did anyone know then, but thanks to former rider Graham Hurry and his team at the Astra Grass-track Club, the sport returned to the Gate Inn raceway at Rhodes Minnis in 2002! The full results from the 1963 Championships were:

Don Godden (29) caught in stylish action.

350cc final – First: Alf Hagon (58.8mph), Second: Denys Goodacre, Third: Don Godden, Fourth: George Markey, Fifth: Gerry Goodwin, Sixth: Jackie Sewell.

500cc final – First: Reg Luckhurst (60.5mph), Second: Alf Hagon, Third: Bill Bridgett, Fourth: George Markey, Fifth: Denys Goodacre, Sixth: Don Godden.

Sidecar final – First: Nigel Mead/Dave Hunter (53.7mph), Second: Bryan Rust/Dave Heath, Third: Mike Webster/John Justice, Fourth: Dave Nourish/J. Curtis, Fifth: John Sykes/Dave Reynolds, Sixth: Derek Yorke/George Mason.

Team Championship (Solo) – First: South-East 61pts, Second: Eastern 54, Equal Third: East Midlands and South Midlands 48, Fifth: Midlands 46, Sixth: Southern 16.

Team Championship (Sidecar) – First: East Midlands 14pts, Second: East Yorkshire 13, Third: Eastern 11, Fourth: South-East, Equal Fifth: Southern and Yorkshire 7.

Unfortunately, with the demise of the Minety Vale Club's track at Long Newnton, there were just two meetings held in the Wessex Centre during the season. These were staged at the Wilts Border Club's circuit at Derriads, near Chippenham, and at a new venue run by the BSSA (Wessex) at Iron Acton, close to Yate, which was to successfully host the sport for ten years.

The meeting at Derriads resulted in a 250cc final success for George Bewley, while Bill Bridgett took victory in both the 500cc final and Experts final. Two finals were also held for the Up to 1,000cc category, with Lew Coffin sweeping all before him for a glorious double. Meanwhile, the remarkable Ken Norcutt gleaned yet another sidecar success in the Unlimited final, finishing ahead of Gordon Gill and Trevor Stuckey. Vintage racing was included in the programme too, with John Glen taking victory on board a 350cc Velocette machine from 1928.

On the 700-yard track at Iron Acton, Lew Coffin was again in great form, winning the BSSA Trophy final and the Unlimited final, although he was defeated in the 350cc event by Dave Langston. In the sidecars no less than three finals were raced, with each resulting in victory for Bristol's Tony Donadel.

Unfortunately, not a lot happened in Gloucestershire, but at least the West Glos & Dean Forest Auto Club ran a mountain-style meeting at St Whites Farm in Cinderford on 7 September. There were mainly scramblers in the line-up, including top exponents Malcolm and Tony Davis, Jim Timms and Mick Burton. The entry was augmented by a few grass-track regulars, however, in Hereford's Brian Leaman and Ken Williams, Pershore's George Bewley, the Perry brothers and Chris Healey from Gloucester, as well as local Coleford rider Trevor Plant. The Wye Valley Auto Club also ran their third annual mountain-style event at Hope under Dinmore one week later when Gerry Goodwin swept the board in the solos while Lawson Crisp was a double sidecar victor.

Staying in the Western Centre, the speedy Lew Coffin defeated George Bewley and Arthur Stuffins to retain the Withington Show Challenge Trophy. Meanwhile the

Gordon Gill and passenger Mike David (100) pictured at a Broadhembury event, 1963.

111

Bill Stanford (11) came from a real grass-track family as his father (Walter) and brother (Bob) also participated in the sport.

Thursday-evening-staged Three Counties Show grass-track event attracted a terrific line-up for the Challenge Cup, including the great Barry Briggs. With a prize of £10 for the winner, other riders in the field included Ray Harris, Mike Watkins, Lew Coffin, Bill Bridgett, Bill Stanford, Trevor Plant, Ron Taylor, Tig and Selwyn Perry, Mick Wilmore, Ivor Lawrence, John Stallworthy and Dave Langston. Results from the meeting were as follows:

> Challenge Cup final – First: Barry Briggs, Second: Ron Taylor, Third: Ray Harris.
> 500cc final – First: Lew Coffin, Second: Bill Bridgett, Third: Mick Wilmore.
> Unlimited final – First: Ron Taylor, Second: Barry Briggs, Third: Lew Coffin.
> 6-Fastest final – First: Ron Taylor, Second: Lew Coffin.

In the South Midlands, the Hayes Club ran at Harlington with a massive sidecar entry of fifty outfits! John Shears, Freddie French and Ray Gerring proved to be the top three drivers, while in the solos Dave Palmer won both the 250cc and 1,000cc finals, with Doug Drewett taking victory in the 350cc class.

There was wonderful news down in Cornwall with an upsurge of interest in the sport. In April, the BSSA (Cornwall) ran its very first event, and was to go on running meetings thereafter for thirty-eight years! That historic initial event saw the Bill Uren and Vic Morris combination take the chequered flag in three sidecar finals, while Adrian Kessell was victorious in the 8-Fastest final.

The BSSA (Cornwall) ran other meetings during the year at both Redruth and Black Cross, near Fraddon. The racing at Redruth was held on the Portreath mountain track, and having seen action from the venue on video, co-author Dave Stallworthy is able to vouch for the fact that it really was quite a circuit! Looking at the programme from Black Cross, sidecar drivers taking part included Ken Westaway, Cedric James, Phil Williams and Eddie Seymour, all of whom would play their part in the history of Cornish grass-track racing. Also in Cornwall, the North Cornwall Motor Club held a Thursday evening meeting at Launceston in July, while the Pendennis Motorcycle & Light Car Club organized racing at Porthleven in August.

Up in the South-Western Centre, grass-track action was witnessed at Yeo Vale (Yeovil), South Molton, Broadhembury (Greenham, near Wellington) and Bridgwater (Cannington). As might have been expected Lew Coffin was the dominant rider at these venues, although he did lose out to Dave Langston in the 250cc final at Greenham. The meeting also featured two men associated with top-level scrambles racing in Don and Derek Rickman. Don, mounted on his Bultaco, took a brace of second places and a third in the finals, while Derek, on board a Metisse machine, came third in the Bob Smith Trophy behind Lew Coffin and brother Don.

In the Midlands, some exciting events included grass-track racing at the Midland Agricultural Show in Shrewsbury, organized by the Salop Motor Club. A classy line-up included Don Godden, Gerry Goodwin and Jack Grindley, but it was the showground specialists Arthur Stuffins and George Bewley who scooped final successes – Stuffins with two wins and Bewley with one. Godden did have the consolation, however, of beating Bewley in the 500cc final.

Don Rickman (74), Don Freemantle (65), Derek Rickman (54) and Colin Henly (55) head the pack at Greenham, 1963.

Staying in the region, Lew Coffin made the trip up-country for a meeting at Brandon, close to Coventry Speedway, where he beat Gerry Goodwin and George Bewley. At the Bewdley Club's event at Cleobury Mortimer, Goodwin proved to be in scintillating form, taking victory in no less than four finals. At Market Drayton, Goodwin was again in great form, winning two finals, with Jack Grindley and Ivor Lawrence also in the placings. At West Brom, Goodwin enjoyed another success in the 350cc final, although Bewley had the upper-hand in all three of the other finals. Turning to the sidecars at this meeting, Bill Evans proved he was still a force to be reckoned with by taking two final victories. At the Saturday evening meeting at Corporation Meadow, Evesham, that man Bewley was again triumphant, taking the flag in the 250cc, Over 300cc and Unlimited finals, but he had to give second best to Ron Taylor in the 350cc category. Meanwhile in the sidecars there was a brace of wins for Ray Gerring. Finally, at the Donnington Show, near Shrewsbury, a young Tom Leadbitter, later of speedway fame, finished third in the 250cc class, mounted on DOT machinery.

Wales, Scotland and Ireland all held race meetings on a regular basis during the year. Carmarthen Park was one of the favourites, and as previously mentioned in this volume, the oval-shaped West Wales circuit was situated around the outside of the town's rugby pitch, with a banked concrete cycle track running around the perimeter. From their vantage point looking down on the action spectators often witnessed successes for Lew Coffin and Ron Taylor at this venue.

At Rhayader in mid-Wales, the annual Whit Monday meeting was dominated by Bill Bridgett, who raced to victory in three finals, each time ahead of Shropshire's Jack Grindley. Also at this event, a race that solely featured local riders was won by the fast-rising Gerald Evans, the year's Welsh Champion. Llanbister was another of the Welsh venues, and Lew Coffin made another of his sorties to win both the 250cc and 500cc finals ahead of Gerry Goodwin. Clearly enjoying an excellent season in the sport, Goodwin reversed those results as he sped to victory ahead of Coffin in the 500cc and Unlimited finals. Thirty-nine years on the two riders met up again, when Gerry was one of the guests at Lew's surprise eightieth birthday party in Yeovil! In the same year (2002), as a mark of the respect in which he is held in Wales, Lew was invited to open the new Carmarthen Speedway circuit at the United Counties Showground on 21 April.

Up in Scotland, Andy Pryde was the 350cc victor at Kirkcaldy ahead of Bill Beattie, while at Perth, he also won two finals, although he did suffer defeat at the hands of the up-and-coming Brian Brown in the Up to 300cc class. Meanwhile in the Novice final, victory went to future British Moto-cross Champion Vic Allan.

The leading riders in Ireland were Gerry Scarlett, along with the JAP-riding duo of Jack Agnew and Eric Williams. While researching this publication co-author Dave Stallworthy spoke with Jack Agnew, who explained that the Irish tracks were not at all like the English ovals. Instead of being pretty rough, they were very fast and a top speed of around 90mph could be reached on the straights.

Eric Williams won the five-mile Southern Centre Championship at Castleconnell, County Limerick, defeating Jack Agnew. Also victorious at the prestigious event was another rider who was to do well on the Irish circuits, namely Declan Swanton (mounted on a Greeves machine) in the 250cc class.

Looking at some of the other areas, Goole's Paul Cross won a couple of finals at Skipton in Yorkshire, while Roger Gibbs from Caulden, Stafford garnered four final successes at Prestwich in Lancashire. Meanwhile, Graham Gibbs (Roger's brother) was victorious in the 500cc final of the Championship meeting run by the Lancashire Grass-Track Riders' Club, with the runner-up spot being filled by a rider who was destined to make a big impact in the sport, namely Dave Baybutt. Third place was filled by Ken Moss, who sadly passed away in the spring of 2003 following an illness. Ken, of course, went on to race for Belle Vue Colts, helping them to lift speedway's Division 2 Championship in both 1968 and 1969 as well as the Knock-Out Cup, also in 1969. Latterly, and before his untimely death, Ken was promoter at Buxton Speedway, a venue regarded by many as one of the most pleasant within grass-track's sister sport.

The aforementioned Lancashire Grass-Track Riders' Club (LGTRC) had been the brainchild of veteran all-rounder Harry Draper, who hailed from Great Eccleston, Chorley. The sport had virtually died in Lancashire and Cheshire, but Draper contacted a few old-timers like Andy Courtney, Jim Baybutt and Harry Terretta, with the upshot being the club's first meeting at High Moor Farm, Wrightington on Good Friday 12 April 1963. Scrambles star Dick Clayton jr and Yorkshireman Paul Cross shared the solo honours, while soon-to-be National Champion Nigel Mead of York beat the locals in the three sidecar events.

Messrs Draper, Courtney, Baybutt and Terretta all had sons who rode grass-track. The best known, of course, were the Baybutt brothers, Dave and Chris, with Dave actually riding in that first meeting at the tender age of just fifteen! A couple of years later Chris began his career at the same age, appearing under the pseudonym of Jack Dean.

The forming of the LGTRC had a knock-on effect; soon several other clubs were formed in the North-West. The legacy of this produced some of the greatest riders ever seen in the UK, namely the likes of Chris Pusey, Steve Hartley, Terry Owen, brothers Tom and Joe Owen, the previously mentioned Baybutt brothers and last but not least the Collins clan – headed by future World Speedway Champion Peter Collins.

At Kingsley, near Northwich in Cheshire, Ron Taylor made the trek up to win three finals, with his main opposition supplied by Gerry Goodwin. Rain threatened to ruin the racing at the Long Sutton Show, but Bill Bridgett mastered the wet conditions to win four of the finals, two of them ahead of Arthur Stuffins. In the sidecars, the leading drivers proved to be the twice victorious Norman Bailey, with Bryan Rust successful in the other final.

In Yorkshire, the Saddleworth Club's event saw brothers Graham and Roger Gibbs collect all the solo winners' trophies between them. Staying in the county, at the Bainbridge Sports Show Mike Webster reigned supreme with a double success in both disciplines (solo and sidecar), while scramblers Alan Lampkin and Norman Crooks also posted solo victories. At Bagby, near Thirsk, Webster (yet again) and Nigel Mead were the winning sidecar drivers, while Jackie Sewell collected a brace of successes in the solos.

Emerging riders like Brian Maxted, Mervyn Price, Dave Castle and Bill Stanford were starting to gain some victories over the more established aces in the East Midlands.

Right: *Bill Bridgett (72) tears around the track.*

Below: *Former scrambler Dave Palmer burns up the circuit at Willoughby Hedge, 1963.*

However, at Sutton, the Ely Club's meeting saw the experienced Denys Goodacre collect a hat-trick of wins, leaving Jackie Sewell to scoop the 250cc final, while sidecar honours were shared between Dave Nourish, Bryan Rust and long-distance traveller Ken Norcutt. In August, the Spalding Club ran an event at Rutland, where Maxted and Castle both celebrated victories. At Leicester's Tilton track, Goodacre plundered no fewer than four final wins, while the sidecar races resulted in a victory apiece for Norcutt and Nourish.

Grass-track racing had proved popular at the Whittlesey Show (Peterborough) in previous years, and 1963 was no exception. The event certainly went well for Wolverhampton Speedway promoter Bill Bridgett, who made the journey from his Staffordshire home to win four finals ahead of locals Arthur Stuffins and Jackie Sewell. At the Peterborough Motorcycle Club's final meeting of the season in October, Stuffins was triumphant in three finals, suffering his only loss to Paul Cross in the third Unlimited event. Meanwhile, with three first places in the sidecars, it also proved a successful meeting for Bryan Rust.

In Nottinghamshire, the Retford & District Motor Club held a prestigious ACU Star round, with Denys Goodacre keeping the honours in the East Midlands by taking both the 350cc and 500cc finals. The results for the event were as follows:

350cc final – First: Denys Goodacre (Hagon), Second: Don Godden (Godden), Third: Alf Hagon (Hagon), Fourth: Jackie Sewell (JAP), Fifth: Reg Nash (Hagon), Sixth: Paul Cross (JAP).

500cc final – First: Denys Goodacre (Hagon), Second: Don Godden (Godden), Third: Alf Hagon (Hagon), Fourth: Jackie Sewell (JAP), Fifth: Paul Cross (JAP), Sixth: Ted Jelf (Hagon).

Sidecar final – First: Ken Norcutt/Brian Peeling (Triumph), Second: Mike Webster/Dave Hunter (Triumph), Third: Dave Nourish/J. Curtis (WHB), Fourth: Nigel Mead/John Justice (Trinor), Fifth: Bryan Rust/Dave Heath (BSA), Sixth: Mick Adams/Brian Munday (Triumph).

Other events in the East Midlands region were held at Witham Marsh Farm (Boston & District Motor Club), Walsoken (Wisbech Club), Crich, near Alfreton (Derwent Motorcycle Club), Clay Lake (Spalding Club), Allsops Lane (Loughborough Club), Ancaster (Grantham Club) and at the Longnor Show (Biggin Motorcycle Club). The list of venues seemed endless, with other events staged at Skegness, Sleaford and Gainsborough.

Top star Ron Taylor was unfortunately involved in a nasty crash at a Sleaford meeting. Thankfully Jack Bennett (whose son Ray was actually riding in the meeting) was in the crowd and as a qualified St John's man, he jumped over the ropes and extricated Ron's tongue from his throat and the soil from his mouth. The heroic Jack then left the stricken rider in the capable hands of Ron Dolby of the St John Ambulance Brigade to successfully give the kiss of life.

Before moving from the area, it is worth mentioning a couple of major events, namely the Cambridgeshire Championships and the Peterborough Show. The latter was run at the East of England Showground, where ever since 1970 regular speedway action has been witnessed. Held on a Thursday evening in July, world stars Jeff Smith and Barry Briggs joined the regular aces in the thick of the action. Smith was destined to take the World 500cc Scrambles Championship in 1964 and 1965, while Briggs had already been crowned World Speedway Champion in 1957 and 1958, and would go on to lift the title on a further two occasions in 1964 and 1966. Smith was actually riding in his first grass-track meeting, and mounted on an Alf Ellis BSA machine he finished fourth in the 350cc final. Victory in that category went to showground expert Arthur Stuffins, although he had to settle for the runner-up position behind 'Briggo' in three Unlimited finals. Meanwhile, looking briefly at the sidecar races, the meeting saw Bryan Rust and Nigel Mead post one win apiece. The Cambridgeshire Championship had not been staged for two years but made a welcome return to the racing calendar. The podium positions were filled in order by Denys Goodacre, Stuffins and Colin Sweby, with South-East driver Brian Stibbs taking the sidecar title.

It was busy in the Southern Centre too, and among the clubs staging racing were Basingstoke, Ringwood, Blackmore Vale, Andover, Salisbury and Alton. At Willoughby Hedge the Blackmore Vale Club ran a National ACU Star round, with the winners being Don Godden (350cc), Lew Coffin (500cc) and Dave Nourish (Sidecar). Staying at the same venue the annual Championships resulted in victories for Dave Palmer (Solo) and Tony Donadel (Sidecar). History was made when the Southern Centre Grass-Track Riders' Association (SCGTRA) were formed, and in 2003 they celebrated their fortieth anniversary.

The Southern Centre Championships were held by the Alton & District Motorcycle Club at Manor Farm, Lasham in Hampshire. Lew Coffin was again triumphant, taking both the 350cc and Up to 1,000cc categories. Unlike in 2002, when Yorkshireman Richard Hall won the 500cc title, back in 1963, the winners had to be residents of the Southern Centre, and although Dave Palmer defeated Coffin in the big final, he wasn't eligible for the title.

There was still plenty of interest in team racing, with several matches taking place. One such meeting was held at the Shaftesbury Showground in September, when Hampshire defeated Dorset 98-94. The victorious outfit were captained by Bert Croucher, the former Southampton Speedway rider and pre-war grass-track favourite, with the side also including Tom Albery, Ray Lambourne, D. Hill-Cousins, Geoff Porter, Colin Henley, C. Exstance and the Holcombe brothers (Frank and Doug). Meanwhile, Dorset were skippered by Lew Coffin, with the rest of the team consisting of Jimmy Gale, John Trevitt, John Stallworthy, Fred and John Saunders, Artie Thick, T. Huntley and Brian Hayter. The sidecar boys were also included in the match, with the top scorers being Harry Bone and J. Barr for Hampshire, and Viv Debben and E. Green for Dorset.

In the Eastern Centre, racing was held at Hanningford (Chelmsford Club), Langford (ESSA), Abridge (Ilford Club), Rayleigh (Southend Club) and Bocking (Braintree Club). There was also a meeting on the first Sunday of December, when the Tigers Club from Grays ran a one-off out-of-season event.

The South-East was another boom area, with many events taking place at various locations, including Pulborough (Horsham Club), Great Chart (Eltham Club), Ashford

(SERA), Rhodes Minnis (Folkestone Club), Westwell (SERA), Ham Farm (Barham Club), Lydden (Astra Club), Ramsgate (Invicta Club), Wootton (GTSA), Rochester Airport (GTSA), Ashford (Eltham Club) and Grafty Green (Maidstone Club). Looking at the programmes, some meetings attracted a massive entry in excess of 100 solos and up to thirty sidecars, while on some occasions more than one event was run on the same day, such was the popularity of the sport in the region! Four of the prestigious Silver Hemet meetings were staged at Wrinsted Court, with the results recorded as follows:

28 April – First: Alf Hagon, Second: Peter Randall, Third: Martin Tatum.
26 May – First: Don Godden, Second: Alf Hagon, Third: Tony Black.
30 June – First: Martin Tatum, Second: Peter Randall, Third: Stuart Mathieson.
28 July – First: Martin Tatum, Second: Tony Black, Third: Stuart Mathieson.

At the Maidstone Aces meeting on 29 June, Eric Colvin finished as runner-up to C. Stratton in the Sidecar Handicap final. Interestingly, Eric Colvin can now be found regularly working on the circuit at Reading Speedway alongside long-time track-man Dougie Harris and, of course, his son Shane appeared in the Racers' team between 1999 and 2003. Going back to the Maidstone Aces of 1963, the event was run in wet conditions, although that didn't stop Tony Black from claiming three final successes, including the Maidstone Championship. Meanwhile, defeating Black in the 500cc final was a young Malcolm Simmons, who went to win the British Speedway Championship in 1976, a year when he later filled second place behind Peter Collins in the World Final.

1963 was certainly a good year for Malcolm Simmons as he also took victory in the Astra TV Trophy ahead of Reg Luckhurst and Alf Hagon. The sidecar event at this meeting resulted in another success for Ken Norcutt, with C. Stratton and Alan Brett occupying the other rostrum positions. Continuing on with the 'Simmo' glory run, at the South-East Championships he won the 250cc, 350cc, 650cc and Individual titles. The results from the meeting run by the Eltham Club were as follows:

200cc final – First: Tony Black, Second: Ted Stokes, Third: Derek Andrews.
250cc final – First: Malcolm Simmons, Second: Ray Whitling, Third: Arthur
    Wicken.
350cc final – First: Malcolm Simmons, Second: Stan Luck, Third: Martin Tatum.
650cc final – First: Malcolm Simmons, Second: Stan Luck, Third: Tony Black.
Individual final – First: Malcolm Simmons, Second: Sid Jarvis, Third: Tony Black.
Sidecar final – First: Ron Young/Bob Penn, Second: C. Stratton/C. Taylor, Third:
    Bert Brett/A. Harvey.

At the ACU Star round, organized by SERA at Westwell in Ashford, it was Reg Luckhurst who came out on top, winning the 500cc final from Don Godden and Jackie Sewell. It was a great day for Luckhurst as he also sped to victory in the 650cc final and the SERA Championship, with Godden claiming first place in the 350cc category ahead of Sewell and Stan Luck. Meanwhile, the other meeting victors were Jackie Sewell (250cc final), Malcolm Simmons (350cc final) and Ken Norcutt/Brian Peeling (Sidecar final).

A famous circuit in the South-East was the fast, oval-shaped one situated at Rochester Airport. This venue attracted top riders and large crowds, especially for an October meeting, which saw a brace of victories each for Don Godden (250cc and 650cc) and Reg Luckhurst (350cc and GTSA Championship), while the main sidecar final was won by the Ron Young/Bob Penn partnership.

Finally, in this look at 1963, it's back to Rhodes Minnis near Folkestone, where the Grand Slam was staged. Needless to say an all-star solo field was assembled for the prestigious event, featuring Barry Briggs, Bjorn Knutsson, Reg Luckhurst, Don Godden, Malcolm Simmons, Sid Jarvis and Stan Luck. The sidecar section also included some of the sport's leading drivers in Norman Bailey, Dave Nourish, Mike Webster, Ken Norcutt and Nigel Mead. Victory in the solos went to Luckhurst (as it had in 1962) from Godden and Simmons, while the sidecar title was scooped by Mead ahead of Webster and Nourish. Sadly, Brian Stibbs (aged twenty-eight) was killed in the sidecar scratch race after being flung from his machine and unavoidably struck by Dave Nourish.

1963 Roll of Honour

National Championships
350cc – Alf Hagon
500cc – Reg Luckhurst
Sidecar – Nigel Mead/Dave Hunter
Inter-Centre Team (Solo) – South-East
Inter-Centre Team (Sidecar) – East Midlands

National ACU Star Championships
350cc and 500cc – Don Godden
Sidecar – Dave Nourish/Tim Harrington

Southern Centre Championships
250cc – Frank Holcombe
350cc and Individual – Lew Coffin
Sidecar – Ken Norcutt/Brian Peeling
Team – Blackmore Vale

South Midlands Centre Championships
125cc – F. Beever
200cc – Mike Gutsell
250cc, 350cc and 500cc – Alf Hagon
Sidecar – Bob Keen
Team – Southall

South-Eastern Centre Championships
200cc – Tony Black
350cc, 650cc and Individual – Malcolm Simmons
Sidecar – Ron Young/Bob Penn

Eastern Centre Championships
250cc – Denis McHarris
350cc – Reg Nash
1,000cc – Ranleigh Attwood
Sidecar – Derek Yorke/George Mason

East Yorkshire Centre Championship
Paul Cross

Welsh Championship
Gerald Evans

Irish Two-Mile Championships
250cc and 350cc – Gerry Scarlett
500cc – Jack Agnew

Worcestershire Championship
Denys Goodacre

Grand Slam
Solo – Reg Luckhurst
Sidecar – Nigel Mead/John Justice

Royal Welsh Show
Bill Bridgett

Cambridgeshire Championships
Solo – Denys Goodacre
Sidecar – Brian Stibbs/Raich Carter

Cornish Sidecar Championship
Bill Uren/Vic Morris

Fordham Trophy
350cc – Don Godden
1,000cc – Denys Goodacre
Sidecar – Ken Norcutt/Brian Peeling

Loughborough Challenge Cup
Denys Goodacre

BSSA Trophy
Lew Coffin

Carnival Kings Sidecar Cup
Ray Gerring/Kevin McCullagh

Willoughby Hedge Championships
Solo – Dave Palmer
Sidecar – Tony Donadel/A. Bird

Withington Show Challenge Trophy
Lew Coffin

Much Marcle Show Challenge Cup
Ray Harris

Whittlesey Show Challenge Cup
Solo – Bill Bridgett
Sidecar – Bryan Rust/Dave Heath

Spalding Golden Helmet Final
Jackie Sewell

Three Counties Show Challenge Cup
Barry Briggs

Richmond Trophy
Denys Goodacre

Sleaford Championship
Denys Goodacre

Ludlow Trophy
Jackie Sewell

Bedford Cup
Ken Norcutt/Brian Peeling

Astra TV Trophy
Solo – Malcolm Simmons
Sidecar – Ken Norcutt/Brian Peeling

Peterborough Show
350cc – Arthur Stuffins
Unlimited – Barry Briggs

Newark & Notts Show
250cc – Arthur Stuffins
500cc and Unlimited – Ron Taylor

Somerset Challenge Shield
Lew Coffin

15
GRASS-TRACK RACING
1964

The year's National Grass-track Championships moved to Lincolnshire, being staged at Thorns Farm, Mareham Lane, Sleaford. The event was organized on behalf of the ACU by the Sleaford & District Motorcycle Club and a large crowd turned out to view the racing on a 900-yard circuit. Those lucky enough to be present witnessed Alf Hagon (350cc) and Reg Luckhurst (500cc) retain the titles they had plundered at Rhodes Minnis the previous year. Turning to the sidecars, no fewer than ten outfits contested the final. After favourites Nigel Mead and Mick Adams had got tangled up at the start victory was to eventually go the way of the Bryan Rust and Dave Heath partnership, ahead of top drivers Norman Bailey and Dave Hunter.

Looking at the solos, Reg Luckhurst defeated fellow South-Easterners Tony Black and Don Godden in the 500cc final. However, he didn't have it all his own way on the day as he was beaten by Brian Maxted in one of the heats. This was a sign of things to come, as Maxted was to go on and emerge as one of the sport's leading lights. Meanwhile, behind Maxted and Luckhurst in the aforementioned heat was another future Champion, namely Lancashire's Dave Baybutt. Turning to the 350cc category, Alf Hagon had to defeat old master Denys Goodacre to take glory, with West Ham's speedway ace Malcolm Simmons in third spot. The major results from the meeting were thus:

350cc final – First: Alf Hagon (Hagon), Second: Denys Goodacre (Hagon), Third: Malcolm Simmons (JAP), Fourth: Tony Black (JAP), Fifth: Arthur Stuffins (RBS), Sixth: Stan Luck (JAP).

500cc final – First: Reg Luckhurst (Lucky JAP), Second: Tony Black (JAP), Third: Don Godden (DG Special), Fourth: Denys Goodacre (Hagon), Fifth: Jackie Sewell (Sewell Special), Sixth: Malcolm Simmons (JAP).

Sidecar final – First: Bryan Rust/Dave Heath (650cc BSA), Second: N. Bailey/ R.D. 'Sparrow' Jackson (650cc Rocbilt), Third: Dave Hunter/Ivan Kitching (650cc Mojo), Fourth: Mick Hamblin/Keith Hamblin (650cc BSA), Fifth: Phil Ball/J. Beck (650cc ML Special), Sixth: Alan Cobb/T. Collins (500cc GRN JAP).

Team Championship (Solo) – First: South-East 80pts, Second: South Midlands 64, Third: East Midlands 61.

Team Championship (Sidecar) – First: Midlands 22pts, Second: East Yorkshire 19, Third: Southern 17.

Multi-National Champion Alf Hagon (350) leading 'Showground King' Arthur Stuffins (289) at the Essex County Show, 1964.

Other top solo names listed in the programme for the prestigious event included Alan Angear, Brian Gladwell, Dave Palmer, Colin Sweby, Lew Coffin, Fred Watts, Gerry Goodwin, Peter Hall, Dave Langston, Roy Oldaker, Ken Moss, Dave Kirby and Martin Tatum. Meanwhile, among the leading sidecar exponents on show were Bert Brett, Jim Waller, Dick Barton, George Cross, Ray Gerring, Terry Pitman, Dave Nourish, Colin Stoneman, Mike Webster, Mick Adams, Lawson Crisp and Harry Bone. It was also interesting to note that the announcer was a Miss V.E. Hazlehurst, as there certainly haven't been too many female commentators on the grass-track scene over the years!

In the South-East, the Folkestone Motorcycle Club were leading the way with major events at their Rhodes Minnis circuit including the Grand Slam on 10 May, the South-Eastern Centre Championships on 9 August and the Southern Television Trophy on 11 October. The Grand Slam had an all-star entry, with the solos featuring the likes of Reg Luckhurst, Malcolm Simmons, Don Godden, Lew Coffin, Stan Luck, Alan Angear, Monty Banks and Tony Black. Also included on the race card was Cornish speedway ace Chris Julian, along with rising stars Ray Cook, Derek Andrews, Martyn Piddock, Colin Packman, Dennis Lemon and Peter Randall. There was an impressive entry list for the sidecars too, with the likes of Ron Waters, Ray Gerring, Dave Lofthouse, Phil Ball, Nigel Mead, Jim Waller and Harry Bone competing. The name of Dave Nourish could also be added as he appeared in both the solos and the sidecars.

The Grand Slam went to Don Godden, who defeated Tony Black and Alf Hagon with an average winning speed of 65.70mph for the ten-lap final. Godden had to work hard for his victory, coming from behind to pass early leader Malcolm Simmons and then Hagon. Meanwhile the victor for the previous three years, Reg Luckhurst, went out after crashing in the 500cc final and then suffered mechanical problems on a machine loaned to him by Monty Banks. It was a good day for Godden though, for as well as his triumph in the Grand Slam he also won the 350cc final and finished third in the 500cc category, behind Hagon and Black. The other solo event for the 250cc class resulted in victory for George Ward on a BSA, while the sidecar title went the way of the Nigel Mead ahead of Eric While. The major results from the prestigious event follow:

250cc final – First: George Ward, Second: Ray Whitling, Third: Chris Stewart.
350cc final – First: Don Godden, Second: Tony Black, Third: Alf Hagon.
500cc final – First: Alf Hagon, Second: Tony Black, Third: Don Godden.
Solo Grand Slam – First: Don Godden, Second: Tony Black, Third: Alf Hagon,
    Fourth: Alan Angear, Fifth: Malcolm Simmons, Sixth: Stan Luck.
Sidecar Scratch final – First: Nigel Mead/Dave Reynolds, Second: Eric
    While/Dave Taylor, Third: Dave Lofthouse/Jon Gabbitas.
Sidecar Grand Slam – First: Nigel Mead/Dave Reynolds, Second: Eric
    While/Dave Taylor, Third: Dave Lofthouse/Jon Gabbitas, Fourth: Alan
    Cobb/Ray Nunn, Fifth: Jim Waller/J. Moate, Sixth: Arthur Wicken/D. Terry.

Prize money for the solo final was £35 for first place, then £20, £12, £8, £4 down to £2 for sixth position. In the sidecars the bounty on offer was £15, £10, £7 10s, £5, £2 10s and £1 5s.

In the South-Eastern Centre Championships Alan Angear had won the 200cc and 650cc categories, and was leading the Blue Riband event for the Unlimited title until being balked. Taking advantage of his misfortune was the 500cc Lucky JAP-mounted Reg Luckhurst, who sped to victory with a race speed of 70.6mph and collected a cash prize of £10. The meeting also saw Graham Banks collect the Richardson Cup for being the best novice on show, while Alf Hagon plundered another brace of trophies in the 250cc and 350cc classes, and Alan Brett took the sidecar title on board a 650cc Tiger. Having said that, the majority of the sidecars were Triumph, Norton or BSA-powered outfits, including several specials, while the bulk of the solo riders were mounted on JAP engines. The major results from the meeting were as follows:

200cc final – First: Alan Angear, Second: Ted Stokes, Third: Chris Stewart.
250cc final – First: Alf Hagon, Second: Chris Stewart, Third: Ted Stokes.
350cc final – First: Alf Hagon, Second: Alan Angear, Third: Martin Tatum.
650cc final – First: Alan Angear, Second: Reg Luckhurst, Third: Alf Hagon.
Unlimited final – First: Reg Luckhurst, Second: Alan Angear, Third: Alf Hagon.
Sidecar final – First: Bert Brett/A. Harvey, Second: Jim Waller/Maurice Wratten,
    Third: Arthur Wicken/C. Smith.

The other big event at Rhodes Minnis was the Southern Television Trophy, although due to a dispute the racing wasn't actually filmed. The trophies were still raced for,

Lew Coffin (22) leads the way from Tig Perry (129) at Iron Acton.

however, with a class field including Barry Briggs, who had lifted the World Speedway Championship for a third time at the Ullevi Stadium in Gothenburg, Sweden exactly one month previously on 11 September. 'Briggo', Reg Luckhurst and Don Godden all took victory in their heats, but it was the latter who went on to garner the prestigious title ahead of Tony Black and Martin Tatum in the final. Turning to the sidecars, it was Yorkshire's Mike Webster who took the honours ahead of Nigel Mead and Dave Nourish. This event witnessed the sidecar debut of former solo rider Arne Hendriksen on a banked outfit called the 'Hinge'. This model, which was to be banned in 1965, was based on a continental-style outfit. Arne certainly caught the eye as he negotiated the right-handed Rhodes Minnis circuit, predominantly on just two wheels!

The South-East had become one of the hotbeds of the sport as a new boom period started to sweep across the UK. At Ashford, the Eltham Championship in May saw Alan Angear sprint to victory from Dave Mitchell. At the Horsham Club's May meeting at Pulborough, there were four final successes for Malcolm Simmons, while Dave Palmer won the 250cc class and Alan Brett completed a sidecar double. Other meetings saw Colin Packman and Chris Stewart star at Crawley, while at Tenterden it was Tony Black who scooped all the major honours. At the Sittingbourne Club's Wrinsted Court raceway Tony Black defeated Sid Jarvis and Ted Stokes to win the September-staged meeting. Meanwhile, Alan Brett, who was known as Bert throughout his racing career, had the beating of John Shears in the sidecar event. Staying in the area, Ramsgate Airport was the venue for an Invicta Club event, which resulted in victories for Malcolm Simmons, Don Godden and Tony Black, with Chris Stewart winning both the 200cc and 250cc events, while Jim Waller took the sidecar title.

The Maidstone Aces Club held a meeting at Grafty Green near Headcorn and this resulted in a treble victory for Alan Angear, with Tony Black romping to success in the other solo final and John Shears winning both sidecar events. Alan Angear also won the 350cc and 500cc ACU National Star rounds at Great Chart, which were run by the Eltham Club. Meanwhile Malcolm Simmons enjoyed more success in the big Barham meeting, his three final victories including the main Championship when he defeated Ted Jelf and Dave Mitchell. Referring to the sidecars once more, John Shears became the first winner of the Brian Stibbs Memorial, receiving for his efforts a special trophy modelled from 79oz of silver by Brian's father.

Another prestigious event in the South-East was run at Rochester Airport in October by the Grass-track Sidecar Association. The line-up included Danish drivers Bo Jensen and Jorgen Momme, with the former dashing to success in both the Scratch and Handicap finals, partnered by Peter Mortensen in the chair. Solo winners on the day were Chris Stewart (250cc), Malcolm Simmons (350cc) and Don Godden (500cc and All-Comers Handicap), with visiting riders Lew Coffin, Dave Palmer and Roy Oldaker adding plenty of extra pep to the meeting.

The Southern Centre Grass-Track Riders' Association (SCGTRA) had been formed the previous year, with the founder members including Lew Coffin, Tom Albery, John Brown, Harry Bone, Alan Harris, Bill Davies, Bert Croucher and John Stallworthy. History was made when the organization then ran its first race meeting at New Milton in Hampshire in 1964. A 26-heat team event took place featuring eight solos and six sidecars per side. The A team, led by Lew Coffin (solos) and Ken Norcutt/Brian Peeling (sidecars) ran out winners by a scoreline of 127 points to 116. Other solo competitors at this meeting included future sidecar man Ken Kenchington, plus Jim Gale, John Saunders, Tom Albery, John Trevitt, Laurie Sims and Artie Thick. Aside from the brilliant Norcutt and Peeling twosome, the sidecar boys were also represented by the combinations of Jack Knight/Dave Thomas, Harry Bone/John Barr, Charlie Rhind-Tutt/Mick Steel, Viv Debben/E. Green, Terry Phillips/D. Whiteborn plus Phil Ball/S. Beck.

There was a lot of track action for fans to see in the South, including showground meetings which were mainly evening-staged events in Dorset and Hampshire. One example was the Royal County Show at Canford near Poole at the end of August, when the Blackmore Vale Club organized the racing on a 400-yard speedway-style oval circuit. Lew Coffin, Fred Watts and Phil Sheppard emerged as the solo winners, while the sidecar events resulted in a brace of victories for Ken Norcutt and one for Dennis Keen.

Prior to that, at the beginning of May the Wimborne Club ran their first grass-track meeting at Eastbury Park, near Blandford. The list of competitors was a good one too, including Colin Sweby, Lew Coffin, John Stallworthy, John Trevitt, Stan Luck, Ray Cross, Peter Jeffery, Peter Swain and Mick Steel. However it was Dave Palmer who took the spoils of victory in three finals, while the exceptional Ken Norcutt and Brian Peeling combination enjoyed a sidecar double.

The year saw many on-track battles between former scrambler Dave Palmer and the amazing Lew Coffin, and the aforementioned meeting at Eastbury Park was no exception, although on that occasion Coffin had to give second best to his younger opponent. The duo were again in combat at the Basingstoke Motorcycle & Light Car Club's event at Harnetts Farm, Heckfield, near Basingstoke, when Palmer again gleaned a hat-trick of successes. Coffin had the consolation of winning the 350cc class, however, while Selwyn Perry and Bill Stanford were also victorious in the 250cc and Novice finals respectively.

Some well-known names at Heckfield included future sidecar aces Mick Cameron and Vic Hiscock, who both took part in the solo races on that occasion. The chair ace of the day was Alan Cobb, with the line-up also featuring 650cc Triumph-mounted novice driver Cecil Taylor, who later went on to become a British Champion. Also competing in the individual classes was Doug Dearden, who raced on a 1928 AJS machine in the vintage class and on ESO equipment in the modern categories.

The National ACU Star rounds for the Southern Centre were run at the Blackmore Vale Club's circuit at Willoughby Hedge in Mere. With both Lew Coffin and Dave Palmer missing the meeting, it was Don Godden who won both the 350cc and 500cc finals, ahead of Colin Sweby and Jackie Sewell respectively, while Trevor and Clive Stuckey emerged triumphant in the sidecars.

The year's Southern Centre Championships were held on Sunday 9 August at East Mills Farm in Fordingbridge. Organized by the Ringwood Motorcycle & Light Car Club on behalf of the Southern Centre ACU, the high-quality event was restricted to competitors who resided within the boundaries of the region. Having said that, riders who had taken part in two other Southern Centre meetings earlier in the season were also permitted to participate!

Lew Coffin fairly steamed to the main Individual title, with Adrian Kessell winning the 350cc class and Blackmore Vale claiming the team trophy. Remarkably it was the seventh time that Coffin had scooped the top prize in the Southern Centre Championships, not to mention it being his fifth successive victory! Among those he defeated on his way to more glory were Peter Randall, Doug Dearden, Roy Oldaker, Richard May, Jim Gale, Fred Watts, Rod Murray, Stan Formhalls, Pat Cousins, Dave Kirby and regular rival Dave Palmer. In the sidecars it was the sensational Ken Norcutt and Brian Peeling combination who beat off the likes of Charlie Rhind-Tutt, Trevor Stuckey, Phil Ball, Jack Knight, Terry Phillips and Ray Gerring to retain the title for a fifth year in a row – just like Coffin in the solos! The sidecar entry also included three passengers who would go on to fame in various disciplines, namely Bruce Carter, Rod Cutler and Roger Measor.

The host club, Ringwood, also ran meetings at the Mount during the year, while the previously mentioned Wimborne Club staged several other events in the region, as did the Kiwi Motorcycle Club and the Salisbury Club.

The Wessex Centre witnessed racing at the popular oval track at Latteridge, near Iron Acton in South Gloucestershire. Here Lew Coffin made a clean sweep in the solos, with the best of the rest being scramblers Len Sanders and Tony Young. Others who did well with either final placings or heat wins were Tom Albery, Tig Perry, Dave Kirby and former Bristol Speedway rider Frank Evans. Meanwhile, mounted on a 500cc Douglas, local rider Roy Nowell was victorious in the Vintage final, with Ray Gerring taking the sidecar honours in both the Experts and Trophy finals. The results from the two major finals of the meeting follow:

Solo Trophy – First: Lew Coffin, Second: Tom Albery, Third: Len Sanders.
Sidecar Trophy – First: Ray Gerring, Second: Trevor Stuckey, Third: Colin
   Stoneman.

An interesting meeting was staged by the Western Speedway Club at Burnt Farm, Corston, near Malmesbury in July, featuring mainly Provincial League speedway riders in a North *v.* South team match, plus a 6-Fastest Riders Handicap race. This was the year that the Provincial League ran outside the jurisdiction of the Speedway Control Board, so it would be correct to say that this meeting was not sanctioned by the ACU. It is worth recording the result though, with the North gaining victory by 59 points to 36 and the scorers thus: North: Bill Bridgett 20, Ray Harris 15, Fred Powell 9, James Bond 8, Chris Harrison 7; South: Peter Vandenberg 13; Pat Wiggins 10; Geoff Mudge 8; Jon Erskine 3; R. Rouf 2. Following that, the 6-Fastest Handicap saw a 1-2-3 for JAP-mounted riders, with Bill Bridgett racing away to win from Ray Harris and Peter Vandenberg.

Still in the Wessex Centre, the Wilts Border Motorcycle & Light Car Club ran a meeting at Chiverlins Farm, Derriads, Chippenham on 21 June. A smooth, speedway-style oval circuit was used, which lent itself to plenty of close racing. Swindon Speedway star Barry Briggs sped to victory in three of the solo finals, with wins also registered by Phil Sheppard in the Novice class, George Bewley in the 250cc category and Adrian Kessell in the 1,000cc Open event. There was sidecar activity too, with a win apiece for Ray Gerring, Ken Norcutt and Cecil Taylor.

There really was an all-star field assembled for this meeting, featuring a host of well-known names from all over the UK. These included Bill and Bob Stanford (from Northamptonshire), Mike Watkins (Leominster), Dave Drinkwater (Evesham), Roy Oldaker (Surrey), Lew Coffin (Sherborne), Martin Tatum (Epsom, Surrey), Alf Hagon (London), Dave Kirby (Watford), Mervyn Price (Raunds, Northamptonshire), Norman Ruddle (Epsom, Surrey), Fred Watts (Crowthorne, Berkshire) and many more. There were several local riders on show, among them Ron Farr (Chippenham), John Stallworthy (Malmesbury), Dudley Witts (Chippenham) and Alan Patis (Swindon). Aside from the solos, there was a massive twenty-seven-outfit sidecar entry and it seemed as though the Wilts Border Club were about to take over from the Minety Vale Club, who had themselves previously taken over as the dominant force from the Highworth Club and before them the West Wilts Club in the area. Full results from the Chiverlins Farm meeting follow:

Novice final – First: Phil Sheppard, Second: Mervyn Hill, Third: Barry Meeks.

250cc final – First: George Bewley, Second: Mervyn Hill, Third: Fred Watts.

350cc final – First: Barry Briggs, Second: Lew Coffin, Third: Roy Oldaker.

500cc final – First: Barry Briggs, Second: Lew Coffin, Third: Alf Hagon.

Experts final – First: Barry Briggs, Second: Lew Coffin, Third: Alf Hagon.

1,000cc Open final – First: Adrian Kessell, Second: Roy Oldaker, Third: Mick Steel.

Sidecar Unlimited final – First: Ray Gerring/Kevin McCullough, Second: Trevor Stuckey/Clive Stuckey.

Sidecar Handicap final – First: Cecil Taylor/F. Eley, Second: Stan Hellyer/F. Bunch, Third: Viv Debben/E.G. Green.

Sidecar Open final – First: Ken Norcutt/Brian Peeling, Second: Ray Gerring/Kevin McCullough, Third: Colin Stoneman/Gerald Stoneman.

Turning to the Western Centre, the Cheltenham Home Guard Club had taken more than a passing interest in the sport by running a meeting at Elmstone Hardwicke. Dave Langston had a triple success, winning the 350cc, 500cc and Unlimited finals, but he had to take second place to Selwyn Perry in the 250cc class. Other riders who did well in the solo categories were Mick Burton on his scrambler, Graham Ing and school-teacher Chris Langlands, while in the sidecars there was a double for Ray Gerring.

At the Ledbury Floral Show, George Bewley defeated Gerry Goodwin and Trevor Plant to land the Challenge Cup, and completing a wonderful day he also raced to victory in the 250cc and 500cc finals, as well as the George Hopkins Challenge Cup. Results from the event were:

250cc final – First: George Bewley, Second: Cyril Jones, Third: Tig Perry.

350cc final – First: Gerry Goodwin, Second: Mervyn Hill, Third: Dave Drinkwater.

500cc final – First: George Bewley, Second: Gerry Goodwin, Third: Fred Thompson.

Floral Challenge Cup – First: George Bewley, Second: Gerry Goodwin, Third: Trevor Plant.

George Hopkins Challenge Cup – First: George Bewley, Second: Bill Stanford, Third: Gerry Goodwin.

Another showground venue brought further glory for George Bewley (on board his 350cc steed) when he swept to a hat-trick of wins over Arthur Stuffins at Much Marcle to take the 500cc final, the show Championship and the Challenge Cup. The sidecar entry included long-time grass-track journalist John Simcock on a Norton, while top Welsh driver Lynn Isaac was mounted on a BSA and also entered the solos on a JAP. The Much Marcle Show had been running since 1883 and although it was reputed that grass-track racing had been included since the 1930s, the authors have only been able to trace results going back to the 1950s. The full title of the event was actually the Much Marcle and Yatton Flower & Sports Show, with the 1964 staging also including horse jumping, the Gloucestershire Regiment Band and a bird display! The grass-track results from this popular show follow:

> 500cc final – First: George Bewley, Second: Arthur Stuffins, Third: Trevor Plant.
> Championship – First: George Bewley, Second: Arthur Stuffins, Third: Ivor Lawrence.
> Challenge Cup – First: George Bewley, Second: Arthur Stuffins, Third: Eddie Wright.
> First Sidecar Open – First: Lawson Crisp, Second: Albert Lewis, Third: Ray Gerring.
> Second Sidecar Open – First: Lawson Crisp, Second: Ray Gerring, Third: Peter Brown.
> Sidecar Handicap – First: Ray Gerring, Second: Peter Brown, Third: Albert Lewis.

The Wye Valley Auto Club, who were responsible for the racing at Much Marcle, also organized an annual mountain-style meeting at Hope under Dinmore, near Hereford. Gerry Goodwin and Mick Burton proved to be the front-runners in the solos, with the latter on board his MBS scrambles bike. Two of the other competitors in the field were also mounted on their scramblers, namely future grass-track ace Adrian Moss, plus Dave Phillips who was later to be involved with the Malvern Club.

Another popular event was the Withington Show, where Lew Coffin had another tremendous day, winning the 350cc, 500cc and Unlimited finals. However it was local man Ron Taylor who sped to victory in the Challenge Trophy final and the Handicap event, restricting Coffin to second position in the former, with Trevor Plant in third spot.

In the South Midlands region, the Vampire Club's August meeting in Middlesex brought solo successes for Derek Andrews, Colin Sweby and Jim Collins, while there were also sidecar wins for Roy Woollard and Derek Yorke. Something which seemed to be catching on were sprint events at St Albans, with regular grass-trackers taking the awards, most notably Peter Randall, Denis McHarris and Roger Elmore in the solos and Mick Adams in the sidecars. Meanwhile, the 880-yard circuit at Abridge was utilized by the Ilford Club and there was a triple solo success for Dave Palmer, with John Skinner also completing a treble in the sidecars.

Dave Palmer was the star of the Farnham Club's meeting at the end of August, although he did suffer defeat in the 12-Fastest Riders' race at the hands of Roy Oldaker. The meeting also saw Colin Sweby register a couple of third-place finishes, while Bristol vintage riders Roy Nowell and Eric Haskins defeated the locals on their 1920s Douglas machines. The Wycombe Club ran several events at their Chiltern Hills circuit in Stokenchurch, including the National ACU Star round in May. The prestigious meeting saw Martin Tatum emerge triumphant from both the 350cc and 500cc classes, with Nigel Mead taking victory ahead of Ken Norcutt in the sidecars.

The Watford Club again staged racing at Cassiobury Park where Dave Palmer took the chequered flag in the 250cc and 1,000cc categories with Colin Sweby winning the 350cc event. However, in the Don Davis Memorial Trophy, Arthur Stuffins defeated both Palmer and Sweby as well as Peter Colver. Later in the season, more action at the venue resulted in final victories for Don Godden, Alf Hagon and Peter Randall.

Alf Hagon was once more to the fore in the South Midlands Championships, held at Charville Lane, Hayes in Middlesex, winning the 250cc and 1,000 titles. The big event also saw success for Roy Oldaker in the 350cc class, while Ray Gerring became Champion in the sidecars.

At the Eastern Centre's National ACU Star round it was Don Godden and Mike Webster who recorded wins on the Bocking circuit, the meeting being organized by the Braintree Club. The results from the day follow:

350cc ACU Star round final – First: Don Godden, Second: Alf Hagon, Third: Roy Oldaker.
500cc ACU Star round final – First: Don Godden, Second: Alan Angear, Third: Alf Hagon.
Sidecar ACU Star round final – First: Mike Webster, Second: Norman Bailey, Third: T. Rumsey.

Alf Hagon continued to add to his long list of career wins when he defeated Arthur Stuffins in three finals at the Essex County Show, with Derek Yorke also racing to a triple success in the sidecar races. Stuffins wasn't the bridesmaid in every event as he did take victory in the 250cc class. Hagon also swept the board at Aldham, near Colchester, defeating fellow aces Colin Sweby, Martin Tatum and Alan Angear, while Dick Barton, who now resides in Devizes, collected a brace of sidecar wins on his BSA outfit.

At the Canewdon track, near Rochford, the Southend Club's meeting saw three wins for Dave Palmer and a couple for Arthur Stuffins, while Derek Yorke dominated the sidecars. Meanwhile, at the Worthing Eagles event, the main winners were Roy Oldaker in the solos and Ron Young in the sidecars.

Moving further up-country, Don Godden made the trip north to Yorkshire for the National ACU Star round at Harwood Dale, near Scarborough. His efforts proved worthwhile too, as he won the 350cc category from Arthur Stuffins and Paul Cross before again leading home Stuffins in the 500cc class, with Dave Baybutt in third place. Meanwhile, on home turf in Yorkshire, Mike Webster was victorious in the sidecars following close races with Nigel Mead and Dave Nourish.

Staying in the area, the Pickering Club event, which is still going strong today, brought three victories for Paul Cross. There was also a win for the BSA-mounted Bob Jackson in the 250cc class, while Dave Hunter took the plaudits for a double success in the two main sidecar finals. At the Hull Auto Club event in August the solo races were dominated by George Chapman, while Dave Hunter was again the top sidecar exponent on show.

Frank Smith, the father of future triple-British Speedway Champion and Grand Prix rider Andy, sped to glory in the East Yorkshire Grass-track Championship ahead of Paul Cross and Bob Jackson. The Bradford Club also organized meetings in the region and their Easter Monday event at Esholt Park saw four different solo victors, with Frank Smith winning the 250cc class and Paul Cross taking the 350cc final. There were also two races for the 1,000cc boys, with a win apiece for Ken Moss and Dave Baybutt.

131

In the North-West, Bob Jackson (Hagon) and scrambler John Griffiths (Greeves) were the main winners at the Potters Motorcycle Sporting Club's Wednesday evening event at Betley, near Crewe. Meanwhile at Helsby, near Chester on a big 1,000-yard oval circuit, Graham Gibbs and Jack Grindley were the solo victors. In Lancashire, a Good Friday meeting at Wrightington proved successful for Paul Cross, Ken Moss, Bob Jackson, Arthur Randles and Roger Gibbs in the solos, while the Tribsa-mounted Eric Castle was a double sidecar winner.

The North Lancashire Club also staged the sport at the Clapham Sports Show, where Bob Jackson and Malcolm Walker were the main winners among the eighteen races held, with Eric Carr and Keith Rylance also registering victories. A Saturday evening meeting at Prestwich resulted in a brace of wins apiece for Graham Gibbs and Bob Jackson, while the following day another event at Wrightington saw youngster Dave Baybutt post a triple success, with Gibbs claiming a solitary victory. Among the other leading solo stars on show were Alan Knapkin and Arthur Randles, while in the sidecars there was a glorious treble for Ray Edge.

Further racing was staged at Scoutshead, near Oldham, where Bob Jackson won the 250cc final and Dave Baybutt emerged victorious ahead of Graham Gibbs in the 500cc version. Keeping it in the family, the Unlimited final resulted in triumph for Dave's father Jim Baybutt, with Gibbs again having to settle for the runner-up position.

The Retford Club's National ACU Star round in Nottinghamshire brought a win for Alf Hagon in the 350cc class, with Denys Goodacre speeding to victory in the 500cc category. The sidecar final had to be rerun after Mike Webster had crashed while dicing for the lead, with Nigel Mead and Dave Reynolds taking victory at the second attempt. The Retford Club also staged the Richmond Trophy at their Leverton Road circuit and this resulted in another triumph for Goodacre, with Jackie Sewell and Dave Baybutt filling the other rostrum positions.

Over the border in Lincolnshire, Denys Goodacre enjoyed a bumper day out to win all the solo finals at Navenby Lowfields in May, while sidecar-great Bryan Rust followed suit in his chosen discipline. In August at Croft, near Skegness, there was a sidecar double for Nigel Mead, with the victorious solo boys being Brian Maxted, Jackie Sewell and John Whitehead.

At the annual Whittlesey Agricultural Show in Cambridgeshire, Arthur Stuffins won three out of the four solo finals, losing out only to George Bewley in the 350cc category. Colin Sweby and Roy Oldaker were the best of the rest in the solos, with Joey Neath the top man in the sidecars thanks to a brace of victories.

Denys Goodacre was still knocking up plenty of wins in 1964 and the former National Champion made a clean sweep at the Derwent Club's Manor Farm track at Dethick in Derbyshire. Indeed, he defeated a whole host of top-line riders, including Paul Cross, Gerry Goodwin, Ken Moss and Jackie Sewell. Meanwhile, at Highfield, the Littleport Club ran the prestigious Ludlow Trophy meeting and Sewell again had to settle for a supporting role as he came home behind a triumphant Arthur Stuffins.

Ludlow Trophy victor Arthur Stuffins had always shown a liking for the showground circuits and the small oval at the Long Sutton Agricultural Show proved no exception as he took victory in all the solo finals on offer. Although everybody was well-beaten by

Midlander Graham Hancox (391) leads from Gerry Wheeler (8).

the showground maestro himself on the day, the likes of George Bewley, Tony Steggles and Paul Cross all featured prominently in the solo results, while Norman Bailey raced to success in both sidecar finals.

The Midland Centre included racing at Ufton in Warwickshire, organized by the Leamington Club. Gerry Goodwin dominated the solos classes at this venue, leaving Dave Langston, George Bewley and Peter Hall to fight for the runner-up places. At least Langston had the consolation of winning the 250cc final, while there were a couple of sidecar victories for Peter Brown and one for Graham Hancox. Meanwhile, winding down his career in the chairs, Bill Evans twice filled podium positions with second and third-place finishes.

At the popular Saturday night Evesham Club event, the solo finals resulted in wins for Dave Langston (250cc), Bill Stanford (350cc), Ron Taylor (500cc) and George Bewley (Unlimited), while there was one win each for top drivers Ray Gerring and Peter Brown in the sidecars. The Redditch Club held racing at Hanbury Park, Droitwich, with the circuit providing a double victory for Ron Taylor, while Dave Langston won the 250cc final ahead of leading Midlands scrambler Ken Sedgeley. The sidecar boys also featured in a full programme of racing, with Ray Edge and Phil Ball registering a win apiece.

Gerry Goodwin in the solos and Peter Brown in the sidecars were the prevailing forces at the Wolverhampton Club's Wrottesley Park meeting. Both dashed to success against an all-star field, with the solo cast featuring the likes of Dave Baybutt, Jack Grindley and scrambler Pat Lamper. Close to Coventry Speedway, the Antelope Club ran an event at Brandon, where George Bewley was clearly in the winning mode as he

Frank Heard (77) heads Peter Jeffery snr (59) at a South Molton Club meeting, 1964.

garnered a hat-trick of final successes. He didn't claim a clean sweep, however, as Ron Taylor defeated him in the Unlimited class, while Bob Jackson was the 250cc victor ahead of future Crewe Speedway rider Barry Meeks. Finally in the area, it was again George Bewley and Gerry Goodwin to the fore in the West Brom Club's meeting at Tamworth, with Dave Nourish being the sidecar star.

The Bridgwater Club were running in the South-West at Edington in Somerset, with Lew Coffin taking the chequered flag in all his finals at the August meeting. Adrian Kessell and Dave Langston were the best of the rest in the solos, while in the sidecars the leading exponents were Ray Gerring with two wins and Algy Simper with a single success.

Throughout the 1960s, both the Bridgwater and Yeo Vale Clubs organized some cracking meetings in the South-Western Centre. Indeed, one of these occurred at Yeovil on the eve of the Blackmore Vale Club-staged Southern Centre National ACU Star Championship round in the next county, when several visitors took on the South-West boys. The solo honours went to Gerry Goodwin in the 250cc final and in the first Unlimited race, with Roy Oldaker and Jackie Sewell taking victory in the two subsequent Unlimited events. In a real share out, there was also a win for Stan Luck in the 8-Fastest final, while in the sidecars Ken Norcutt completed a double and Ray Gerring was victorious in the other such race. Running through the list of winners there was obviously plenty of stiff opposition, with the best performers among the West Country speedsters being Adrian Kessell in the solos and Trevor Stuckey in the sidecars.

Adrian Kessell was in inspired form over at the Taunton Club's event at Ashill, winning all of his races, with the other leading riders on the day being Tom Albery, Ray

Lambourne and Peter Jeffery snr. It was a different story for Kessell at the South Molton Club's July meeting, however, as he was outgunned by the amazingly consistent Lew Coffin. Looking at the sidecars it was a good day for both Trevor Stuckey and Colin Stoneman as they each posted two victories. Also in the South-West, at Tiverton, Coffin again got the better of Kessell, with Ken Norcutt and Gordon Gill being the sidecar winners. Vintage races were also featured in a meeting that provided something for everyone, with Roy Nowell and Eric Haskins posting a win apiece on their 500cc Douglas machines.

Ken Norcutt and Colin Stoneman were again sidecar winners at the Broadhembury event, while in the solos Ron Taylor made a fruitful foray to win three finals, with Adrian Kessell taking the 250cc category. A particularly good field assembled for this meeting, with a number of leading riders present such as Pat Cousins, Dave Threadingham, Denny Belcher and Tom Albery. Briefly referring back to the Bridgwater Club, they also ran at Spaxton, including an October event which saw solo victories for George Bewley, Fred Watts and Ron Taylor, with success in the sidecars for Gordon Gill and Trevor Stuckey. In a link with the present day, Spaxton is of course where they now race in the modern era.

In Cornwall, racing was held by the BSSA Club at both Portreath and Hayle. More often than not it was Adrian Kessell and Chris Julian who came out on top in the solo categories, while the top sidecar drivers were Cedric James, Bill Uren, Eddie Seymour and Phil Williams.

Over in West Wales, the Carmarthen Club were again busy and once more ran a meeting at the famous Carmarthen Park circuit. Ron Taylor was the undisputed man of the day, defeating George Bewley and K.W. Jones for a triple solo success in the 500cc, Unlimited and 6-Fastest finals. Alan Cobb enjoyed himself in the sidecars with a brace of final wins, and there was at least some consolation for the duo who filled the minor podium positions in the solo events as Bewley had the beating of Tom Albery to win the 350cc final, while Jones took the 250cc final ahead of Bewley and Trevor Plant.

At Builth Wells on Easter Monday, Ron Taylor won both the 500cc and Unlimited finals, while Cyril Jones also enjoyed a brace of victories by taking the chequered flag in the 250cc and Local Riders' categories. Spreading the trophies around, there was also glory for Gerald Evans in the 350cc class ahead of George Bewley and Cyril Jones.

Lew Coffin made the trek up to North Wales to compete in the Aberystwyth Club's event at Blaendolau Park. The effort proved worthwhile as he took the spoils of victory in the 350cc final. However he then had to settle for the runner-up position in the 500cc and Unlimited classes as Ron Taylor completed a double success. Completing the winners on the day was Vic Madeley, who finished ahead of the field in the Local Riders' race.

Ron Taylor again showed his liking for the Principality circuits with another two wins in the Teme Vale meeting at Knucklas, organized by the Central Wales Auto Club. George Bewley also recorded a couple of victories on the day while Gerry Goodwin took the 250cc final. Turning to the sidecars, there was a victory apiece for top drivers Lawson Crisp and Peter Brown. In an incident-packed event, there was certainly much for the spectators to enthuse over as the solo line-up also featured the likes of Tig Perry, Arthur Randles, Jack Grindley, Ivor Lawrence and Cyril Jones.

At the Trefaldwyn Motorcycle Club's meeting at Kerry, near Newtown, the solo honours went to Gerry Goodwin (250cc and 350cc finals), Dave Baybutt (Unlimited final) and Gerald Evans (Non-Winners final), while Lawson Crisp added to his list of victories with a sidecar double.

Up in Scotland, there was a triple solo success for Perth rider Ian Coutts in the Scottish Championship round at Forfar, with Andy Pryde following him home in all three.

There was plenty of action in Ireland throughout the year, with those competing using mainly scrambles-style machines. At Carrickfergus the solo winners included Jack Agnew, Willie Johnston and Mervyn McConkey, while Noel Bell and Brian Nally took runner-up placings. Down in the South the Fingal Motor Club ran its first event at Swords, Co. Dublin on 9 August, with Brian Nally collecting a brace of victories on board his JAP.

At Comber, Co. Down, Mervyn McConkey won the 350cc and 500cc Irish Ten-Mile Championship races, while leading road-racer Tommy Robb made a return to the sport to take the 200cc class. At Donaghadee, also in Co. Down, the Bedford Cup featured wins for George Bowden, Norman Gray and Brian Kelly. In Dublin, there was a double success for Mervyn McConkey in the National Championships as he crossed the line ahead in the 350cc Five Mile event and also in the 500cc Two Mile class, with Willie Johnston taking victory in the 200cc Two Mile category.

Briefly running through some of the other race meetings in Ireland, there were two final wins for the Greeves-mounted Declan Swanton at the East Cork Club's meeting at Middleton. Meanwhile at Straffan, Co. Dublin, it was a day to remember for Eric Williams as he posted a hat-trick of victories mounted on his JAP. At the West Cork Club's circuit at Dunmanway, Jim Porter snr raced away to triumph in the Cork Examiner Cup, while Joe Moran was victorious in two of the day's other events. The Irish Motorcycle Club held a meeting at Athy, where David Long, Gerry Scarlett and Douglas Pearson all garnered final wins. Finally, at Lisburn, Davey Mills, Gordon Bell, Willie Johnston and John Cunningham all tasted victory.

Overall, grass-track racing had reached an even greater level of popularity in 1964, and it is almost impossible to recount all the events that were held during the year. Suffice to say that thousands of races were staged throughout the UK and a wonderful twenty-year period of growth had begun, led by a batch of youngsters who had started to make a name for themselves, most notably Graham Banks and Dave Baybutt.

1964 Roll of Honour

National Championships
350cc – Alf Hagon
500cc – Reg Luckhurst
Sidecar – Bryan Rust/Dave Heath
Inter-Centre Team (Solo) – South-East
Inter-Centre Team (Sidecar) – Midlands

National ACU Star Championships
350cc and 500cc – Don Godden
Sidecar – Nigel Mead/Dave Reynolds

Southern Centre Championships
250cc – Dave Palmer
350cc – Adrian Kessell
Individual – Lew Coffin
Sidecar – Ken Norcutt/Brian Peeling
Team – Blackmore Vale

Southern Centre Star Championships
250cc and 500cc – Dave Palmer
Sidecar – Ken Norcutt/Brian Peeling

South Midlands Centre Championships
200cc – John Argrave
250cc and 1,000cc – Alf Hagon
350cc – Roy Oldaker
Sidecar – Ray Gerring/Kevin McCullagh

South-Eastern Centre Championships
200cc and 650cc – Alan Angear
250cc and 350cc – Alf Hagon
Individual – Reg Luckhurst
Sidecar – Bert Brett/A. Harvey

Eastern Centre Championships
250cc, 350cc and 1,000cc – Alf Hagon
Sidecar – Dick Barton/D.A. Pearse

East Yorkshire Champion
Frank Smith

Irish Championships
200cc (Two miles) – Willie Johnston
200cc (Ten miles) – Tommy Robb
250cc (Ten miles) – Norman Gray
350cc and 500cc (Two miles) – Mervyn
McConkey
350cc and 500cc (Five miles) – Mervyn
McConkey
350cc and 500cc (Ten miles) – Mervyn
McConkey
Sidecar (Ten miles) – J.W. Parkinson

Scottish Championships
Over 300cc – Andy Pryde
Sidecar – D. Stewart

Worcestershire Championship
Denys Goodacre

Grand Slam
Solo – Don Godden
Sidecar – Nigel Mead/Dave Reynolds

Cornish Sidecar Championship
Bill Uren/Vic Morris

Fordham Trophy
350cc and 1,000cc – Alf Hagon
Sidecar – Mick Adams/Brian Munday

BSSA Trophy
Lew Coffin

Carnival Kings Sidecar Cup
Ray Gerring/Kevin McCullagh

Withington Show Challenge Trophy
Ron Taylor

North-East Cheshire Show Trophy
Bob Jackson

Ely Show Challenge Cup
Solo – Arthur Stuffins
Sidecar – Mick Adams/Brian Munday

Essex County Show
Solo – Alf Hagon
Sidecar – Derek Yorke/J. Chisnall

Much Marcle Show Challenge Cup
George Bewley

Whittlesey Show Challenge Cup
Solo – Arthur Stuffins
Sidecar – Joey Neath/D. Crick

Spalding Golden Helmet Final
Jackie Sewell

Three Counties Show Challenge Cup
Ron Taylor

Long Sutton Show Challenge Cup
Solo – Arthur Stuffins
Sidecar – Norman Bailey/R.D. Jackson

Bosbury Show Challenge Trophy
Ron Taylor

Ledbury Show Challenge Cup
George Bewley

Ludlow Trophy
Arthur Stuffins

Bedford Cup
Bryan Rust/Dave Heath

Dave Bach Memorial Left-Hand Sidecar Trophy
Ron Young/Bob Penn

Bert Smythe Left-Hand Sidecar Trophy
Ron Young/Bob Penn

Richmond Trophy
Denys Goodacre

Cambridgeshire Show
Arthur Stuffins

Newark & Notts Show
250cc and Unlimited – Arthur Stuffins
350cc – Ken Moss
500cc – Ron Taylor

Royal Counties Show
350cc – Lew Coffin
500cc – Fred Watts
Sidecar – Ken Norcutt/Brian Peeling

Peterborough Show
Solo – Arthur Stuffins
Sidecar – Norman Bailey/R.D. Jackson

Brian Stibbs Left-Hand Sidecar Memorial Trophy
Ron Waters/Graham Croucher

Southern TV Trophy
Solo – Don Godden
Sidecar – Mike Webster/John Justice

Don Davis Memorial Trophy
Arthur Stuffins

16
GRASS-TRACK RACING
1965

The National Championships moved to the Eastern Centre and the Lyons Hall Farm at Bocking, near Braintree in Essex, where an estimated audience of 20,000 viewed the action on Sunday 5 September. Organized by the Braintree & District Motorcycle Club on behalf of the ACU, the meeting saw the solo categories dominated by the men from the South-East who filled the top three places in each class. The 350cc final brought a first victory for Tony Black ahead of Don Godden, with Malcolm Simmons occupying the other rostrum position. Meanwhile, Godden raced away on the 880-yard circuit to become the 500cc Champion, with Stan Luck taking second place from 1964-victor Reg Luckhurst. Twenty-nine-year-old Godden hailed from Maidstone in Kent and was certainly the rider in peak form in the mid-1960s, although Black at three years his junior and teenage sensation Simmons were also pushing for the top. Add to these riders like Luckhurst, Alan Angear and many more and it was clear to see why the South-East boys were the ones to beat in the solo races.

Both solo categories saw the rise of some of the new names on the scene, most notably Chris Stewart, Peter Randall and Brian Maxted. Outside the top six, but still qualifying for the finals, however, were many of the sport's more established riders such as Mervyn Price, Martin Tatum, Dave Palmer, Arthur Stuffins, Brian Gladwell, Dave Baybutt, Lew Coffin, Roy Oldaker, Jackie Sewell, Adrian Kessell, Reg Nash, Ken Moss and Richard May.

Drivers from Yorkshire and the East Midlands regions dominated the sidecar section of the programme, with the Dave Hunter and Ivan Kitching combination taking the title from Mike Webster and his partner John Justice. As had been expected, the South-East team won the solo Inter-Centre Championship, with Godden, Simmons, Luckhurst and Stuffins winning the 350cc races, while 500cc victories were registered by Hagon, Simmons, Godden and Price. Meanwhile, courtesy of wins from Webster, Nigel Mead and Dave Lofthouse, the sidecar title went the way of East Yorkshire. The results from the big event follow:

350cc final – First: Tony Black (Hagon JAP), Second: Don Godden (DGS JAP), Third: Malcolm Simmons (Hagon JAP), Fourth: Chris Stewart (Hagon JAP), Fifth: Jackie Sewell (Sewell JAP), Sixth: Peter Randall (Hagon JAP).

500cc final – First: Don Godden (DGS JAP), Second: Stan Luck (Hagon JAP), Third: Reg Luckhurst (Lucky JAP), Fourth: Brian Maxted (Elstar JAP), Fifth: Malcolm Simmons (Hagon JAP), Sixth: Alf Hagon (Hagon JAP).

Sidecar final – First: Dave Hunter/Ivan Kitching (Mojo Triumph), Second: Mike Webster/John Justice (Triumph), Third: Dave Nourish/Tim Harrington (WHB Triumph), Fourth: Dave Lofthouse/Eddie Crawford (Triumph), Fifth: Roger Dutton/Jim Miller (Triumph), Sixth: Norman Bailey/D. Smith (Rocbilt Triumph).

Team Championship (Solo) – First: South-East 47pts, Second: East Midlands 41, Third: Eastern 35, Fourth: South Midlands 32, Fifth: Southern 26, Sixth: East Yorkshire 21.

Team Championship (Sidecar) – First: East Yorkshire 20pts, Second: East Midlands 18, Third: Eastern 15, Fourth: Yorkshire XX, Equal Fifth: Southern, South-West and South-East 12.

Down in the South-West, the Bridgwater Club ran two meetings at Edington, with one staged on Easter Monday and the other in October. For the latter event a massive field of over fifty sidecars entered, with Graham Hancox victorious in both the Unlimited and Experts finals, while Cecil Taylor won the Handicap race and Don 'Nobby' Golden took the Junior category. There was an all-star cast for the solo events, with Lew Coffin posting a treble success to add to his many other career wins. The day's solo results were:

350cc final – First: Lew Coffin, Second: Cyril Jones, Third: Adrian Kessell.
500cc final – First: Lew Coffin, Second: Tim Bungay, Third: George Bewley.
Junior final – First: John Webb, Second: J. Knight, Third: R. Kelly.
Experts final – First: Lew Coffin, Second: George Bewley, Third: Cyril Jones.
Unlimited final – First: John Webb, Second: Tim Bungay, Third: Cyril Jones.
12-Fastest final – First: George Bewley, Second: Adrian Kessell, Third: Pat Cousins.

The big event in the region was the National ACU Star round at Parshalls Farm in Donyatt, near Ilminster, which was staged by the Broadhembury & District Motor Club on 11 July. A high-quality entry list were faced with a wet track for the meeting, although Lew Coffin made light of the conditions to beat Arthur Stuffins across the line in the 350cc class. However, Coffin was later disqualified for course-cutting, with Stuffins subsequently awarded the winner's prize of £12. In the 500cc category it was Bill Bridgett who scooped the first prize of £17, while Mike Webster was the happy recipient of £20 in the sidecar event. The main results were:

350cc ACU Star round final – First: Arthur Stuffins, Second: Tony Black, Third: Bill Bridgett.
500cc ACU Star round final – First: Bill Bridgett, Second: Arthur Stuffins, Third: Lew Coffin.
Sidecar ACU Star round final – First: Mike Webster/John Justice, Second: Gordon Gill/Mike David, Third: Trevor Stuckey/Clive Stuckey.

The meeting also featured several other races, with the results as follows:

250cc solos – First: Peter Jeffery, Second: Bill Davies, Third: Adrian Kessell.
350cc solos – First: Arthur Stuffins, Second: Bill Bridgett, Third: Lew Coffin.
500cc solos – First: Bill Bridgett, Second: Lew Coffin, Third: Phil Sheppard.
Invitation solos – First: Bill Bridgett, Second: Lew Coffin, Third: Phil Sheppard.
Up to 1,300cc sidecars – First: Mike Webster/John Justice, Second: Trevor Stuckey/Clive Stuckey, Third: Terry Weedy/M. Weeby.
Handical sidecars – First: Mike Webster/John Justice, Second: Trevor Stuckey/Clive Stuckey, Third: Gordon Gill/Mike David.

Aside from those already mentioned, to emphasize just how good the field was the solo events also featured Laurie Sims, Terry Major, John Trevitt, John Stallworthy, Barry Wade, Fred Saunders, Doug Dearden, Gerry Goodwin and Stan Luck. Looking in a little more detail at the sidecar boys, among the other drivers were the likes of John Browne, Gilbert Bedford, Terry Pitman, Ron MacBeth, Terry Skinner, Dennis Quick and Viv Debben.

Lew Coffin was at his brilliant best on home turf at the Yeo Vale Motorcycle Club's meeting at Five Ashes, Higher Odcombe, Yeovil on 25 July, taking victory in all the solo finals. The event formed a round of the South-Western Centre Championships and making sure all the trophies went to the locals, the sidecar finals were won by the BSA-mounted twosome of Gordon Gill and Mike David. On a busy day of racing there was also a solo team match included in the programme and this saw the South defeat the Midlands by 64 points to 27. The teams were made up as follows: South: Lew Coffin (Captain), John Knight, John Stallworthy, John Trevitt, Alan Harris, Tom Albery and Peter Jeffery; Midlands: Bill Davies (Captain), George Brashaw, Harry Badger, Ivor Lawrence, Dave Drinkwater, J. Slater and G. Taylor.

Further down the country in Cornwall a full season of racing was run by the BSSA Club, with meetings held on 18 April, 9 May, 18 July, 15 August and 12 September, while the North Cornwall Club also staged an event on 25 July. Solo racers Adrian Kessell and Terry Major were two of the leading lights in the area, with Eric Perryman beginning to make his mark. In the sidecars, the top drivers were Cedric James, Bill Uren, Phil Williams, Eddie Seymour and John Hammill. Meanwhile, at Zelah, near Newquay, the final meeting of the season saw St Austell's Ken Westaway start on the ladder of success by defeating Seymour in the Non-Winners final, mounted on board his Triton outfit.

On 20 August, Ron Taylor was taking victory in all the solo finals at the Central Wales Auto Club's meeting at the Teme Vale circuit. Taylor was again very successful in the Welsh events throughout the year, winning finals at the Park in Carmarthen, Stepaside (near Tenby) and Aberystwyth. However, he didn't have it all his own way as he finished as runner-up to George Bewley at the Builth Wells-staged Royal Welsh Show. Before moving on from the Principality it is worth mentioning the grass-track racing at the Llanfyllin Show which was dominated by Cyril Jones, with that man Taylor having to settle for three runner-up placings. The results follow:

350cc final – First: Cyril Jones, Second: Ron Taylor, Third: Ivor Smart.

500cc final – First: Cyril Jones, Second: Ron Taylor, Third: Terry Challinor.

Unlimited final – First: Cyril Jones, Second: Ron Taylor, Third: Gerald Evans.

In the Wessex Centre just four meetings were held during the year, one apiece by the Wilts Border Club, BSSA, Bristol Motorcycle & Light Car Club and the Frome & District Motorcycle and Light Car Club. Looking more closely at the Wilts Border Club's event which took place at Corsham on 9 May, the solo honours were shared out among Dave Palmer (250cc final), Roy Oldaker (350cc final), Ron Taylor (First Experts final) and Bill Bridgett (Second Experts final). In what was some line-up, Taylor also won the Up to 1,000cc class ahead of Bridgett, Lew Coffin, Palmer, Ray Harris and George Bewley, with Phil Ball and Ken Norcutt being the main sidecar victors.

At Latteridge Green Farm, Iron Acton, near Yate on 1 August, Lew Coffin dominated the proceedings with four solo victories on a superb oval circuit. The results were recorded thus:

350cc Open – First: Lew Coffin, Second: John Stallworthy, Third: Adrian Kessell, Fourth: Pat Cousins, Fifth: Peter Jeffery, Sixth: Tig Perry.

500cc Open – First: Lew Coffin, Second: Adrian Kessell, Third: Tig Perry, Fourth: Peter Jeffery, Fifth: Tom Albery, Sixth: Barry Wade.

BSSA Trophy – First: Lew Coffin, Second: Tig Perry, Third: Adrian Kessell, Fourth: Tom Albery, Fifth: Peter Jeffery, Sixth: Dave Threadingham.

12-Fastest Riders – First: Lew Coffin, Second: Tig Perry, Third: Adrian Kessell, Fourth: Peter Jeffery, Fifth: John Stallworthy, Sixth: Dave Kirby.

Juniors – First: Tig Perry, Second: J. Taylor, Third: Chris Langlands, Fourth: Pat Cousins, Fifth: Dave Threadingham, Sixth: Dave Kirby.

The sidecar races featured two victories for Gerald Stoneman and a win each for Gordon Gill and Trevor Stuckey, while Adrian Kessell took the chequered flag in both solo vintage events on board the 1926 Zenith machine which his father, Tommy, had used when winning the Cornish Championship in 1933.

The Bristol meeting took place at Old Sodbury on 21 August and was a bit different to the norm as it included not only the usual solos and sidecars, but also vintage races and seven different car classes. Among those racing the cars was renowned photographer Gordon Francis in an Austin Cooper S, and when he wasn't burning up the circuit he was busy taking pictures of the action! Due to the varied programme there weren't many solo races, with the top riders being Dave Threadington on his 500cc Metisse scrambler and regular grasser Tom Albery.

The last event of the Wessex season took place in Frome, but wasn't that successful due to heavy rain. The solo riders who adapted best to the muddy conditions, however, were Dave Langston and Adrian Kessell, with Chris Langlands posting a double of Novice final victories. In the sidecars the honours were shared by Gordon Gill, Henry Body and Gerry Wheeler.

South-West greats Lew Coffin (22) and Adrian Kessell (5) in combat at Iron Acton, 1965.

As usual the Evesham Motorcycle Club held the Worcestershire Championship for solo racers and the Carnival King's Cup for the sidecar boys at Ham Dean Farm, Pinvin, near Pershore. Former cinder-shifter and Wolverhampton Speedway co-promoter Bill Bridgett was in sparkling form, taking victory in the Over 300cc and 350cc races at the famous track, and in the eight-lap Worcestershire Championship none of the other competitors could get near him. In the other races there was a 250cc success for Dave Langston, while the Mick Adams and Brian Munday combination came out on top in the sidecars after dicing with the Ray Gerring and Kevin McCullagh partnership. The results follow:

Worcestershire Championship – First: Bill Bridgett, Second: Lew Coffin, Third: Cyril Jones, Fourth: George Bewley, Fifth: Dave Langston, Sixth: Mervyn Hill.
250cc solos – First: Dave Langston, Second: Cyril Jones, Third: George Bewley, Fourth: Tig Perry, Fifth: Bill Davies, Sixth: Terry Bird.
Over 300cc solos – First: Bill Bridgett, Second: Lew Coffin, Third: Cyril Jones, Fourth: George Bewley, Fifth: Peter Hall, Sixth: Mervyn Hill.
350cc solos – First: Bill Bridgett, Second: Lew Coffin, Third: Dave Langston, Fourth: Colin Davenport, Fifth: Dave Drinkwater, Sixth: Terry Bird.
Carnival King's Cup – First: Mick Adams/Brian Munday, Second: Ray Gerring/Kevin McCullagh, Third: John Cork/N. Bellmy, Fourth: J. Chapman/ D. Quirk, Fifth: Albert Lewis/Roy Whiteley, Sixth: P. Guise/G. Barham.
Up to 700cc sidecars – First: Mick Adams/Brian Munday, Second: Ray Gerring/Kevin McCullagh, Third: Graham Hancox/P. Sheasby, Fourth: John Cork/N. Bellmy, Fifth: Vic Artus/Alan Artus, Sixth: Albert Lewis/Roy Whiteley.

Tony Donadel and partner Alan Bird (25) racing at Old Sodbury, 1965.

Brothers Trevor and Clive Stuckey (4) in action at the Mount, 1965.

In September the Evesham Club ran another meeting at Honeybourne and this brought solo final victories for Cyril Jones (250cc), Ivor Lawrence (over 300cc) and George Bewley (350cc and Unlimited), while in the sidecars there were a couple of wins for Peter Pithie and one for Lawson Crisp.

Other Midlands meetings included one run by the Redditch Club on their Hanbury circuit near Droitwich, where Gerry Goodwin was in dominant mood, winning all four solo finals. Moving from two wheels to three, the 500-yard track served up plenty of thrills with Mick Adams and Albert Lewis winning one race apiece to share the honours. At Leamington, there were two solo final victories each for Dave Langston and Tig Perry, while the sidecars ended in solitary successes for Vic Artus and Graham Hancox. At West Brom, Bill Bridgett added more trophies to his collection with a hat-trick of solo wins to his name, while Cyril Jones gleaned a 250cc victory ahead of Mervyn Hill. The meeting also served up some exciting sidecar action, with Peter Pithie and John Cork each recording a win.

Coventry's Antelope Club organized meetings in April, June and August, with Bill Bridgett the star at all three. At the April event there was a rare appearance on grass from Coventry Speedway ace Nigel Boocock on board a 500cc Triumph. The England international didn't do too badly either, running a fourth place in the Unlimited final behind Bill Bridgett, local club rider Peter Hall and Ron Taylor. Sidecar legend Bill Evans also had a rare outing in the meeting, collecting two third-place finishes in the sidecar finals.

In the Southern Centre Dave Palmer was victorious in three solo finals at the Farnham meeting in July, with Stan Luck winning the 350cc class. The sidecars saw the Gordon Gill and Mike David combination register an impressive double, while a vintage three-team event resulted in a win for London ahead of Bristol and Exeter. Treble-victor Palmer was also a winner of many other finals in the region during the year, including events run by the following clubs: Wimborne (Whitchurch), Ringwood (Fordingbridge), Portsmouth (Petersfield), Salisbury (Ansty) and Ringwood (the Mount).

The Centre Championships were organized by the Kiwi Motorcycle Club and staged at Westover Farm, near Andover. Although Dave Palmer added to his list of wins in the 250cc category ahead of Peter Jeffery and Barry Meeks, it was the remarkable Lew Coffin who sped home to take both the 350cc and Individual titles. Turning to the sidecars there was yet another success for the magical Ken Norcutt, with Phil Ball and Terry Pitman occupying the other podium positions. The full results from the big meeting were as follows:

250cc final – First: Dave Palmer, Second: Peter Jeffery, Third: Barry Meeks, Fourth: Fred Watts.

350cc final – First: Lew Coffin, Second: Richard May, Third: Adrian Kessell, Fourth: Fred Watts.

Individual final (351-1,000cc) – First: Lew Coffin, Second: Dave Palmer, Third: Richard May, Fourth: Peter Randall, Fifth: Doug Dearden, Sixth: Mick Steel.

Sidecar final – First: Ken Norcutt/Brian Peeling, Second: Phil Ball/J. Beck, Third: Terry Pitman/W. Woodward, Fourth: Charlie Rhind-Tutt/P. Coles.

Lew Coffin and John Stallworthy pictured with a German banking-sidecar outfit.

Somewhat fittingly the team shield was won by the Southern Centre Grass-Track Riders' Association (SCGTRA) and although they were not listed as Championship events, other winners from the day included Chris Steel (Over 350cc Novice and Unlimited Novice), Lew Coffin (Over 350cc Star) and Ken Norcutt (Sidecar Star).

Having mentioned the SCGTRA, they ran a meeting at Came Park near Dorchester in aid of the Police Convalescent Home on Saturday 11 September, when both the Lord Lieutenant of Dorset and the Chief Constable were present to witness the proceedings. The track was a tiny speedway-style oval, which best suited Lew Coffin, Barry Meeks and John Stallworthy. Indeed, Stallworthy enjoyed the best meeting of his racing career, completing a double success in the 500cc and 8-Fastest finals. He had to accept second best to Coffin, however, in the 350cc and Experts finals, but could be well-satisfied with his efforts. The Police Trophy was awarded on the basis of aggregate points attained during the meeting, and with Meeks taking victory in the 250cc and Novice classes, as well as finishing as runner-up in the 500cc category, it was he who was declared the winner. Phil Ball certainly had a day to remember too, as he recorded a trio of sidecar victories in the Open, Invitation and Experts classes. Full results from a very busy programme of events follow:

> 250cc final – First: Barry Meeks, Second: Kevin McCullagh, Third: Bill Davies.
> 350cc final – First: Lew Coffin, Second: John Stallworthy, Third: Kevin McCullagh.

500cc final – First: John Stallworthy, Second: Barry Meeks, Third: Kevin McCullagh.

Experts final – First: Lew Coffin, Second: John Stallworthy, Third: Tom Albery.

8-Fastest final – First: John Stallworthy, Second: Lew Coffin, Third: Stan Formhalls.

Novice final – First: Barry Meeks, Second: Kevin McCullagh, Third: Alan Harris.

Vintage final – First: Pat Cousins, Second: Lew Coffin.

Sidecar Open final – First: Phil Ball/J. Beck, Second: Harry Bone/J. Barr, Third: Gordon Gill/Mike David.

Sidecar Invitation final – First: Phil Ball/J. Beck, Second: Gordon Gill/Mike David, Third: Charlie Rhind-Tutt/P. Coles.

Sidecar Experts final – First: Phil Ball/J. Beck, Second: Gordon Gill/Mike David, Third: Charlie Rhind-Tutt/P. Coles.

Sidecar Experts Barred final – First: Don Golden/John Miell, Second: Ken O'Hare/J. Davies, Third: Ron Cutler/J. Hayter.

The Wimborne Club also ran a meeting at Tarrant Gunville near Blandford and it was Adrian Kessell's turn to shine as he posted two wins to lift both the Committee Trophy and the Fastest Time of the Day Trophy. Other successes at the event saw John Saunders pick up the Ronald Farquharson Shield for winning the Novice final ahead of Peter

John Stallworthy being presented with the SCGTRA Trophy at Dorchester, 1965.

Jeffery, while Ken Henbest took the chequered flag in the Experts final and there were victories too for Ken Norcutt and Terry Pitman in the sidecar races.

Aside from the main two riders in the area, Lew Coffin and Dave Palmer, other leading solo track merchants included a pair of brothers in Mick and Chris Steel and John and Fred Saunders, plus Tim Bungay, Richard May, Doug Dearden and youngster Pat Cousins.

The long-established Blackmore Vale Club had now moved to a new circuit at Capps Lane, Westbury in Wiltshire and they organized two events during the year. The first took place on a cold and windy day on 18 April, when Dave Palmer was the best of the solo performers despite running a second to Northamptonshire's Bill Stanford in the 350cc class. Meanwhile Charlie Rhind-Tutt was the top sidecar exponent at a meeting which had a rare visit from former grass-tracker Glyn Chandler, who had chosen to concentrate on the sister sport of speedway. It wasn't a memorable day out for the Swindon-born racer, however, as he was beset with problems caused by mechanical gremlins.

Later in the season the Blackmore Vale Championships took place at the same venue on 30 August, when several other speedway riders made a rare appearance on grass, including Frank Shuter, Mike Cake, Peter Swain and Pete Munday. However, having made the long trek south, it was established grasser Arthur Stuffins who beat all the other aces to take home the Bain Trophy and the Blackmore Vale Championship. Also featuring in the solo results were the likes of Dave Langston, Lew Coffin and Adrian Kessell, while the sidecar honours were split between Graham Hancox, Gordon Gill, Tony Smith and Dennis Quick.

Don Godden dominated the 350cc and 500cc ACU Star races at Blackmore Vale's Mere circuit, while local driver Dennis Keen won the sidecar class. This was the last round of the series and the final overall placings resulted in triumph for Tony Black (350cc), Godden (500cc) and Mike Webster (Sidecar). The leading overall positions follow:

> 350cc National ACU Star Championship – First: Tony Black, Second: Don Godden, Third: Dave Baybutt, Fourth: Arthur Stuffins, Fifth: Stan Luck, Sixth: Malcolm Simmons.
> 500cc National ACU Star Championship – First: Don Godden, Second: Tony Black, Third: Dave Baybutt, Fourth: Stan Luck, Fifth: Brian Maxted, Equal Sixth: Reg Luckhurst, Arthur Stuffins and Malcolm Simmons.
> Sidecar National ACU Star Championship – First: Mike Webster, Second: Dave Hunter, Third: Roger Dutton, Fourth: Dave Lofthouse, Fifth: Nigel Mead, Sixth: Gordon Gill.

A new club to hold a one-off meeting in the Western Centre was the Cirencester Motorcycle Club. Their event was run at Sisters Farm, Cricklade Road, South Cerney on 15 August and attracted a good field which included Hereford scrambler Randy Owen, who is better known nowadays as a sponsor, through his Owen Brothers business, of Grand Prix star Leigh Adams. A double victory went the way of Ron Taylor in the 500cc and Unlimited finals, but he only managed third place in the 350cc category behind Lew Coffin and Peter Jeffery. The other classes in an exciting meeting resulted in a 250cc win for Tig Perry, with John Cork and Gordon Gill each posting a sidecar success.

Staying in the Western Centre, the Wye Valley Auto Club again held a mountain-style event at Hope under Dinmore near Hereford. In the solos Gerry Goodwin collected two final wins, while Ron Taylor had a solitary success, although scrambler Mick Burton is worthy of great praise as he pushed them all the way. Looking at the sidecars, there was a brace of victories for Ray Gerring and one for Bristol's Dennis Quick.

Between them the Wye Valley Auto Club and the Ross Club were responsible for organizing most of the Western Centre's fantastic showground events. The year's Withington Show Challenge Trophy went the way of Ron Taylor ahead of George Bewley and Ray Harris. On another day to savour, Taylor also claimed the 350cc and 8-Fastest finals, while Lew Coffin defeated the spectacular Trevor Plant and the evergreen Harris to take the 500cc class. The story was the same at Much Marcle, where Taylor again prevailed to take three trophies. The results were as follows:

500cc Hereford Challenge Race – First: Ron Taylor, Second: George Bewley, Third: Lew Coffin.

Open Championship – First: Ron Taylor, Second: George Bewley, Third: Lew Coffin.

Much Marcle Challenge Cup – First: Ron Taylor, Second: Lew Coffin, Third: George Bewley.

A good selection of riders were present for this event and aside from the leading trio of Taylor, Coffin and Bewley, the line-up included Noel Clark, Peter Hall, Mervyn Hill, Ivor Lawrence, Dave Langston, Trevor Plant, John Stallworthy, Tig Perry, Tom Albery, Colin Davenport, John Webb and Vic Madeley, plus brothers Bill and Bob Stanford. There were also two other interesting names among the competitors, the first being scrambler Randy Owen, who changed from his conventional equipment and competed on a 500cc grass machine. The other was the then Stonehouse-based Adrian Moss on board a 250cc Cotton scrambler, and of course he would later go on to be the organizer of the present day British Pre-75 Championships. Most of the showground meetings were restricted to just solo riders, but they did have the sidecar outfits at Much Marcle, with one victory apiece going to Gordon Gill and Dennis Quick.

There was no halting Ron Taylor at the showground meetings as he also recorded a triple success at the Grafton Show at the Ashe, Much Birch, near Hereford. He did, however, get off to a bad start in the Up to 1,000cc final, which let in George Bewley to take the flag from John Webb. It was a great day for the latter named Webb, for that was one of three runner-up finishes the former scrambler claimed on board his 500cc JAP. Forty-five-year-old Ray Harris was again in action at the meeting, but after winning various heats and semi-finals the best he could manage in the finals was a third place in the 500cc category behind Taylor and Webb.

John Webb is, of course, still a regular at oval-track meetings nowadays as his daughter is married to American speedway ace Brent Werner, who has enjoyed a career

Arthur Stuffins (2) and Graham Gibbs (49) crash spectacularly at a Sleaford meeting, 1965.

in domestic British racing with several teams: Long Eaton (1995-97), Newcastle (1998), Workington (1999-00), Eastbourne (2001) and Rye House (2002-04), while he also doubled-up with Peterborough in 2003. John also still has a major interest in the grass scene through his involvement with the new Worcestershire Grass-track Club. Harking back to 1965, John certainly had one of his best-ever races when he defeated Ron Taylor and Dave Langston at the Cheltenham Home Guard's meeting at Boddington in August.

The Ross club had also run a non-showground event on a 500-yard oval track in April, when George Bewley, Ron Taylor and Bill Bridgett shared out the victories, with the likes of Mick Burton, Bill Stanford, Randy Owen and Selwyn Perry taking top-three placings.

The Three Counties Show at Malvern gave Lew Coffin a treble victory in the 350cc, Unlimited and Challenge Cup finals, but he had to settle for second spot behind Ron Taylor in the 6-Fastest Riders' race. The results from this prestigious event follow:

350cc final – First: Lew Coffin, Second: Bill Bridgett, Third: Ron Taylor.
Unlimited final – First: Lew Coffin, Second: Bill Bridgett, Third: Ray Harris.
Challenge Cup final – First: Lew Coffin, Second: Ron Taylor, Third: Bill Bridgett.
6-Fastest Riders' final – First: Ron Taylor, Second: Lew Coffin, Third: Bill
    Bridgett.

The East Midlands region was still producing some first-class race meetings, including the Derwent Club's May event at Shuckstone Farm near Matlock, which saw star visitor from Lancashire, Dave Baybutt, triumph in four solo finals. Among the best of the rest, meanwhile, were Coventry's Peter Hall, the Gibbs brothers (Roger and Graham), Cheshire's Ken Terretta (the brother of Keith, who was tragically killed in a car accident in 1960) and Joe Hughes.

Also in May, the Grantham Pegasus Motorcycle & Light Car Club hosted racing on a 750-yard circuit at Woodnook in Lincolnshire. An estimated 2,000 crowd watched Dave Lofthouse and Dave Hunter excel in the sidecars, while Jackie Sewell dominated the solo proceedings, with his main opposition supplied by Mervyn Price, Andy Ross and Bill Stanford.

The Newark Club's August meeting at Brant Broughton produced solo final wins for Gerry Goodwin (250cc), Roger Gibbs (350cc) and Brian Maxted (12-Fastest and Unlimited). Sidecar races were also featured on the agenda and these resulted in a win each for Robin Williamson and Dave Nourish. In the same month the Wisbech Club held an event at Murrow and the day belonged to Arthur Stuffins who posted three final successes, with Mervyn Price (250cc) and Paul Cross (350cc) being the other solo victors. Meanwhile, in the sidecars there was again a win apiece for Williamson and Nourish.

Another meeting at Brant Broughton emphasized just how competitive the area was as there were different solo final winners in John Whitehead (250cc) and Pip Watkin (350cc), while Brian Maxted again took victory in both the 500cc and Unlimited classes. Dave Nourish also collected another sidecar win, with the other race proving successful for Dave Hunter.

There was quite a list of meetings in the area during the year and among others the venues included Swineshead (Boston & District Motorcycle Club), Blyton (Gainsborough & District Motorcycle Club), Hartington (Biggin Motorcycle Club), Tilton (Leicester Club), Clay Lake Field (Spalding & Tongue Auto Club), Allsops Lane (Loughborough & District Motorcycle Club), Mareham Lane (Sleaford & District Motorcycle Club) and Leverton Road (Retford & District Motorcycle Club).

Two of the major showground meetings were held by the Peterborough and Newark Clubs at the agricultural shows. The latter event saw Arthur Stuffins win three finals, while Mervyn Price landed the 250cc category and Bill Stanford was victorious in the 350cc class. At Peterborough there was a star-studded line-up featuring the Stanford brothers, Bill Barley, Tony Steggles, Dave Kirby, Andy Ross, father and son duo Ken and Richard Greer, Mervyn Hill and the just-starting-out Denny Barber, who later went on to make grass-track frames. However, it was Barry Briggs who came out on top in two finals, with Stuffins registering a solitary success.

Staying in the East Midlands, the third round of the National ACU Star Championship was staged at Sleaford and saw Tony Black extend his overall lead in both the 350cc and 500cc classes. On the day, Dave Baybutt took victory in the 350cc category and at 500cc level there was glory for Brian Maxted from Tony Black, Baybutt and Paul Cross, with the sidecars resulting in a win for Dave Hunter over fellow Yorkshire driver and Star points leader Mike Webster.

Moving on to the South Midlands, the Centre Championships were held by the Hayes Club and resulted in a big win for Martin Tatum, while Dave Palmer and Roy Oldaker also registered category successes. It was top honours for Tatum though as he found the quickest way around the Charville Lane circuit in Hayes to triumph in the Up to 1,000cc class. Full results from the event were as follows:

125cc final – First: S. Benn, Second: M. Beenham, Third: G. Newson.
200cc final – First: Denis McHarris, Second: Norman Earis, Third: Brian White.
250cc final – First: Dave Palmer, Second: Denis McHarris, Third: B. Coles.
350cc final – First: Roy Oldaker, Second: John Argrave, Third: Jake Rennison.
Up to 1,000cc final – First: Martin Tatum, Second: Dave Palmer, Third: Roy Oldaker.
Sidecar final – First: Roy Woollard, Second: G. Ford, Third: Ray Geering.

The sad news from the region was that on 11 July the Wycombe Club organized the last-ever meeting at the Chiltern Hills circuit in Stokenchurch.

The Eastern Centre Championships were organized by the Castle Colchester Club and held at Hightrees Farm, West Bergholt in Suffolk. This prestigious event saw multi-Champion Alf Hagon win the 400-1,000cc title, while Jack Hubbard and Colin Flexman put their names to the 250cc and 350cc categories respectively. The sidecars, meanwhile, resulted in triumph for Roger Dutton and his partner Jim Miller.

Another event in the region was the Worthing Eagles meeting in August, when Ray Cook, Roy Oldaker and scrambler Graham Beamish featured among the winners. Earlier in the season the Eastern Sporting Sidecar Association (ESSA) held an event at Little Leighs, where the solo honours were shared between Arthur Stuffins, Roy Oldaker, Colin Packman, Reg Nash and Brian Gladwell, while both sidecar races were won by Derek Yorke. A further ESSA meeting at Langford saw Denis McHarris win the 250cc Cornell Challenge Trophy, while Derek Andrews lifted the Ashby Challenge Cup and Jack Hubbard scooped the Nobby Clarke Challenge Cup.

A top entry closed the season in the Eastern Centre at the Castle Colchester Club's circuit at Hightrees Farm in West Bergholt with Dave Palmer and Tony Black winning the solo finals, while Dave Hunter and John Cork took victory in the main sidecar races. Other solo racers to post top-three placings in the meeting were Stan Luck, Mervyn Price, Jack Hubbard, Jake Rennison and Jackie Sewell.

Before moving on from the Eastern Centre it is worth noting that the Braintree Club had earlier played host to the first round of the ACU Star Championship at Lyons Hall, Bocking. This event was dominated by Don Godden who posted victories in both the 350cc and 500cc finals ahead of Tony Black and Stan Luck. Turning to three wheels, Dick Barton nearly pulled off a shock by leading the way, but he was overhauled by eventual victor Roger Dutton before unfortunately pulling out with a puncture.

As usual there was plenty of action in the North, stretching right across from the east to the west. The East Yorkshire Solo Championship was held by the Hull Auto Club at Wawne, near Beverley, with local rider George Chapman winning the title ahead of Bob Jackson and Geoff Pugsley. There was consolation for the third-placed Pugsley, however, as he enjoyed several successes over the year including victories at the Northallerton Club's event at Bedale.

Among other results in Yorkshire there were solo wins for Mervyn Price at Thirsk, with Dave Hunter to the fore in the sidecars. At Steeton, the Craven Motor Club's meeting resulted in more solo success for Price, with Ken Moss also collecting a final victory. At Pickering, the solo winners included Paul Cross, Geoff Pugsley and George Chapman, while at the Bainbridge Show there was a sidecar double for the versatile Mike Webster, who also took the chequered flag in the 250cc solo class.

Over in the North-West, the Wrexham Club ran a meeting at Holt, with Fred Jackson, George Bewley and Ron Taylor collecting victories, while at the North Lancs Club's track at Quay Meadow there was a clean sweep for Dave Baybutt. At Runcorn, Arthur Randles won three solo finals at a July meeting, while at Prestwich it was Baybutt and Graham Gibbs who sped to success. The year was marred, however, by the loss of Paul Cross, who sadly died following a crash while practising at Wetherby.

In Scotland the prospects certainly looked good in the solo categories with the rise of Andy Ross, together with regulars like Andy Pryde and speedway riders Bill Landels and George Hunter, as well as the up-and-coming talents of Ian McPherson and Brian Brown. The Scottish lads didn't have everything their own way though as Dave Baybutt and Bob Jackson travelled up from the North-West to win some of the finals at the Fife Phoenix Motorcycle Club meeting.

Racing was still popular in Ireland, where Gerry Scarlett and Eric Williams were the main men to beat, with other top riders including Brian Nally, Douglas Pearson and John Kelly.

To finish this look around the country, we come back down to England to cover just some of the fantastic action that accounted for the area known as the South-Eastern Centre. Earlier in the review of the year it was evident just how good the boys from the South-East were on the National scene, but in their own back yard they were almost invincible.

The season started with the GTSA's Rochester Airport meeting at the end of March, when a superb field included Barry Briggs, Arthur Stuffins, Don Godden, Tony Black, Jackie Sewell, Reg Luckhurst and Malcolm Simmons. It was 'Simmo' who proved to be the man 'on the gas' as he sped victory in the Championship final at an average speed of 58.20mph for the twelve-lap race. The West Ham Speedway ace also won the 350cc final ahead of Sewell and defeated Godden in a special match race too! Other winners in the season's opener were Chris Stewart and Tony Black in the 250cc final and Handicap final respectively, while Arthur Wicken won the Sidecar Scratch final and Bill Waters landed the Sidecar Handicap final. The results of the two main solo finals were:

> 350cc final (Six laps) – First: Malcolm Simmons, Second: Jackie Sewell, Third: Don Godden, Fourth: Tony Black, Fifth: Stan Luck, Sixth: Alan Angear.
> Championship final (Twelve laps) – First: Malcolm Simmons, Second: Tony Black, Third: Don Godden, Fourth: Stan Luck, Fifth: Peter Randall, Sixth: Arthur Stuffins.

At the Folkestone Championship it was Stan Luck's turn to shine as he raced away to win the main title from Reg Luckhurst and Tony Black, clocking an average speed of

Right: *Dave Baybutt (26) heads Arthur Stuffins (2) at Wetherby, 1965.*

Below: *Scotland's Ian McPherson (9) leads from Gerry Goodwin (7), Arthur Stuffins (2) and Dave Baybutt (26) at Wetherby, 1965.*

66.30mph as he did so. There was consolation for the other two podium finishers, however, as Black took victory in the 250cc and 350cc events, while Luckhurst scooped the 500cc category. The sidecar races proved most successful for visitors to the area, with Midlands drivers Graham Hancox and Mick Adams to the fore, along with Southerner Phil Ball, while the best of the locals were Jim Waller and Charlie Coleman.

The aforementioned Alan Angear had one of his best results of the season at the Sittingbourne Club's Silver Helmet meeting in June when he not only won the coveted helmet from Peter Randall and Colin Packman but also took the 250cc and 350cc finals. The event also featured a 650cc final win for Randall, while Ron Waters enjoyed a double sidecar success.

The annual South-Eastern Centre Championships were staged by SERA at Malthouse Farm, Great Chart, near Ashford on Sunday 1 August. It proved to be a great day for Wimbledon Speedway heat-leader and keen country and western singer Reg Luckhurst, as he won the Blue Riband Unlimited Championship ahead of an all-star field. The full results from this prestigious event were as follows:

> 200cc final – First: Graham Banks, Second: Ted Stokes, Third: Norman Atkins, Fourth: Brian Nevill, Fifth: Norman Earis, Sixth: R. Hague.
>
> 250cc final – First: Tony Black, Second: Derek Andrews, Third: Chris Stewart, Fourth: Colin Packman, Fifth: Ray Whitling, Sixth: D. Tarrant.
>
> 350cc final – First: Don Godden, Second: Martin Tatum, Third: Dave Mitchell, Fourth: Ray Cook, Fifth: P. Chittenden, Sixth: Derek Andrews.
>
> 650cc final – First: Don Godden, Second: Tony Black, Third: Peter Randall, Fourth: Sid Jarvis, Fifth: Ted Stokes, Sixth: Dave Mitchell.
>
> Unlimited Championship final – First: Reg Luckhurst, Second: Tony Black, Third: Don Godden, Fourth: Martin Tatum, Fifth: Stan Luck, Sixth: Dave Mitchell.
>
> Sidecar final – First: Ron Waters, Second: Bill Waters, Third: Tony Duke, Fourth: R. Taylor, Fifth: Dave Aungier, Sixth: Alan Martin.

It certainly was a quality line-up for the event as aside from those already listed in the results the solo boys included Peter Colver, Dennis Lemon, Mick Cameron, Monty Banks, John Britcher, Ivor Thomas, Jack Appleby, Jake Rennison, Charlie Sharp and John Strickland. The sidecar entry was equally impressive and also featured Mick Saunders, Arthur Wicken, Roy Woollard, Rick Colvin, Steve Holland and future solo rider Alan Barton.

The National ACU Star meeting for the region was organized by the Astra Motorcycle Club and held on 29 August at Parsonage Farm, Stockbury, near Sittingbourne. The top prize for both the 350cc and 500cc finals was £10, while the sidecar victors received a £12 purse for their clockwise (right-handed) efforts. However, the non-Championship sidecar races were run in an anti-clockwise (left-handed) direction! Leading exponents of the sport were very adaptable though and the likes of Charlie Coleman, Arthur Wicken and Jim Waller were equally adept at right-handed or left-handed racing.

The solo winners on the day were Tony Black and Malcolm Simmons in the 350cc and 500cc classes respectively, while Yorkshire's Mike Webster came out on top in the sidecars. Meanwhile, the non-Championship races included a 250cc win for Dave Baybutt, while rising star John Britcher took victory in the 340-1,000cc final. The main results from the event follow:

> 350cc National ACU Star Championship – First: Tony Black, Second: Stan Luck, Third: Jackie Sewell, Fourth: Chris Stewart, Fifth: Martin Tatum, Sixth: Ray Cook.
>
> 500cc National ACU Star Championship – First: Malcolm Simmons, Second: Reg Luckhurst, Third: Stan Luck, Fourth: Alf Hagon, Fifth: Sid Jarvis, Sixth: Colin Packman.
>
> Sidecar National ACU Star Championship – First: Mike Webster/John Justice, Second: Roger Dutton/Jim Miller, Third: Jim Waller/D. Andrews, Fourth: Arthur Wicken/B. Smith, Fifth: Charlie Coleman/M. Fridd, Sixth: Tom Wilson/D. Brewer.

The year's Grand Slam at the Gate Inn circuit in Rhodes Minnis near Folkestone took place right at the end of the season on Sunday 24 October, organized as usual by the Folkestone Motorcycle Club. As well as the leading South-East solo boys, the various visitors included Tony Steggles and Brian Gladwell from the Eastern Centre, Lew Coffin from the South-West, Barry Meeks from the South Midlands and Jackie Sewell from the East Midlands. Meanwhile, from the Midlands, Nigel Boocock was due to make an appearance, but he was replaced by Gerry Goodwin. The sidecar section was also well represented with the drivers from other areas including Graham Hancox, Ray Gerring, John Cork, Peter Pithie, Dave Nourish, Mick Adams, Dave Hunter, Dave Lofthouse, Ron MacBeth, Mike Webster, Vic Artus, Roger Dutton and Phil Ball. It was clearly some field of entrants and read more like a 'Who's Who' of grass-track in 1965!

On board his 500cc Lucky JAP, the great Reg Luckhurst covered the eight-lap distance to retain his Grand Slam title ahead of Tony Black and Peter Randall in a speed of 66.70mph. The sidecars were dominated by Mike Webster, who clocked a speed of 61.70mph in defeating fellow Yorkshire driver Dave Hunter over the six-lap final. In a link with the modern era, Webster is of course the father of multi-Road Race Champion sidecar driver Steve. The main results from the event looked like this:

> Grand Slam (solos) – First: Reg Luckhurst, Second: Tony Black, Third: Peter Randall, Fourth: Stan Luck, Fifth: Monty Banks, Sixth: Mervyn Price, Seventh: Lew Coffin, Eighth: Alan Angear.
>
> Grand Slam (sidecars) – First: Mike Webster/John Justice, Second: Dave Hunter/Ivan Kitching, Third: Dave Lofthouse/Eddie Crawford, Fourth: John Cork/Nev Bellamy, Fifth: Graham Hancox/P. Shearsby, Sixth: Roger Dutton/Jim Miller, Seventh: Peter Pithie/B. Woodward.

Other winners at this end-of-season classic were Black (250cc final), Luck (350cc final), Luckhurst (500cc final) and Webster (Sidecar Scratch final).

For supporters who never previously got the chance to see racing at Rhodes Minnis, a top rider from the 1970s, Graham Hurry, brought racing back to the site in 2002 with the help of his team, and the following year co-author Dave Stallworthy was invited to do some commentating and was simply blown away by what he described as one of the best tracks he had ever seen. Who should be one of the past masters giving a superb demonstration at the 2003 event? None other than the 1965 winner Reg Luckhurst!

That covers the major meetings in the region, but among many other venues racing was witnessed at Crouchers Field, Westwell (SERA), Wallett Court, Headcorn (Maidstone Aces Motorcycle Club), Ham Farm, Barham, near Dover (Barham & District Motorcycle and Light Car Club), Stockbury (Astra Club), Rochester Airport (OWLS Motor Club), Arran's Farm, Bredhurst, near Gillingham (GTSA), Chilmington Green, Great Chart, Ashford (Eltham & District Club), Marden Carnival (Tenterden Club), Wagstaff Farm, Biddenden (Frittenden Club) and Worplesdon, near Guildford (Witley Club).

There are a couple of interesting stories before finishing with 1965. Arne Hendriksen's 'Hinge' outfit was banned, with the officials ruling that only combinations with rigidly fixed sidecars may compete. They did also state that if any individual promoter should like to organize an event solely for hinged three-wheelers they could do so, but needless to say this never occurred! In this wander through the grass-track years the authors have purposely steered away from the mechanical advancements of the sport. However, there might be a few readers wondering what happened to the 'Hinge' and the answer is that it is still in Arne Hendriksen's possession and he still occasionally brings it out for demonstration events.

Danish Sidecar Champions Erik Kestebo and Bob Jensen raced in Kent, while a very famous TT and World Road-Racing star competed in the solos at a South-East grass-track meeting, namely Bill Ivy. 'Little Bill' will be remembered for his titanic battles against Phil Read on their 125cc and 250cc Yamahas in 1968. Tragically, the great little racer was later to lose his life in a racing crash.

As this second volume draws to a close, the emergence of new names was evident with riders like Ray Cook from Stumps Green in Sussex, Bill Hayward from Marden, Martyn Piddock from Ashford, Tig Perry from Gloucester, John Webb from Worcester and Richard May from Southampton. Add to these speedsters like Andy Ross, John Britcher, Gerald Evans, Cyril Jones, Brian Maxted, Ken Moss, Richard Greer, Ian McPherson, Brian Brown and several other up-and-coming young solos plus a booming sidecar class, and the sport clearly looked in good shape going into the late 1960s and beyond.

1965 Roll of Honour

National Championships
350cc – Tony Black
500cc – Don Godden
Sidecar – Dave Hunter/Ivan Kitching
Inter-Centre Team (Solo) – South-East
Inter-Centre Team (Sidecar) – East Yorkshire

National ACU Star Championships
350cc – Tony Black
500cc – Don Godden
Sidecar – Mike Webster/John Justice

Southern Centre Championships
250cc – Dave Palmer
350cc and Individual – Lew Coffin
Sidecar – Ken Norcutt/Brian Peeling
Team – SCGTRA

South Midlands Centre Championships
125cc – S. Benn
200cc – Denis McHarris
250cc – Dave Palmer
350cc – Roy Oldaker
500cc – Martin Tatum
Sidecar – Roy Woollard/Eddie Gypps
Team – Southall

South-Eastern Centre Championships
200cc – Graham Banks
250cc – Tony Black
350cc and 650cc – Don Godden
Individual – Reg Luckhurst
Sidecar – Ron Waters/Graham Croucher

South-Western Centre Championships
350cc and 500cc – Lew Coffin
Sidecar – Trevor Stuckey/Colin Stuckey

Eastern Centre Championships
250cc – Jack Hubbard
350cc – Colin Flexman
1,000cc – Alf Hagon
Sidecar – Roger Dutton/Jim Miller

North-Western Centre Championships
250cc and 500cc – Dave Baybutt
Sidecar – Kevin O'Rourke/N. Douglass

Cheshire Centre Championships
Solo – Dave Baybutt
Sidecar – Kevin O'Rourke/N. Douglass

East Yorkshire Champion
George Chapman

East Midlands Centre Team Championship
Derby Phoenix

Scottish Championships
Up to 300cc – Brian Brown
Over 300cc – J.J. Allen
Sidecar – J.W. Miller

Welsh Championship
Cyril Jones

Irish Two-Mile Championship
Gerry Scarlett

Worcestershire Championship
Bill Bridgett

Grand Slam
Solo – Reg Luckhurst
Sidecar – Mike Webster/John Justice

Cornish Sidecar Championship
Cedric James/Ken Pollard

Blackmore Vale Championships
Solo – Arthur Stuffins
Sidecar – Graham Hancox/P. Shearsby

Bridgwater Trophy
Lew Coffin

Fordham Trophy
350cc – Bill Bridgett
Fastest Riders' – Jackie Sewell
Sidecar – Dave Hunter/Ivan Kitching

BSSA Trophy
Lew Coffin

Carnival Kings Sidecar Cup
Mick Adams/Brian Munday

Royal Counties Show
Lew Coffin

Withington Show Challenge Trophy
Ron Taylor

Essex County Show
Solo – Chris Stewart
Sidecar – Roger Dutton/Jim Miller

Royal Welsh Show
Solo – George Bewley
Sidecar – Lyn Isaac

Much Marcle Show Challenge Cup
Ron Taylor

Whittlesey Show Challenge Cup
Bill Bridgett

Spalding Golden Helmet Final
Brian Maxted

Three Counties Show Challenge Cup
Lew Coffin

Bosbury Show Challenge Trophy
George Bewley

Shrewsbury Show Challenge Cup
Terry Challinor & Cyril Jones (joint-first)

Peterborough Show Challenge Cup
Barry Briggs

Llanfyllin Show Challenge Cup
Cyril Jones

Dave Bach Memorial Left-Hand Sidecar Trophy
Ron Young/Bob Penn

Bert Smythe Left-Hand Sidecar Trophy
Mick Saunders/Ken Temple

Richmond Trophy
Ken Moss

West Midland Show
250cc – Arthur Stuffins
350cc, 500cc and Unlimited – Ron Taylor

Newark & Notts Show
250cc – Mervyn Price
350cc – Bill Stanford
500cc and Unlimited – Arthur Stuffins

Brian Stibbs Left-Hand Sidecar Memorial Trophy
Mick Fletcher/Dave Walters

Don Davis Memorial Trophy
Dave Palmer

St Paul's Trophy
Dave Palmer

Angus Challenge Shield
Tony Black

BSSA Vintage Trophy
Adrian Kessell

Rochester Airport Championship
Malcolm Simmons

Wisbech Clarke Challenge Trophy
Arthur Stuffins

Wisbech Southgate Sidecar Cup
Dave Nourish/Tim Harrington

SCGTRA Trophy
John Stallworthy

If you are interested in purchasing
other books published by Tempus, or in case you have
difficulty finding any Tempus books in your local bookshop,
you can also place orders directly through our website

www.tempus-publishing.com